SADDLEBACK
PUBLISHING·INC.

PRACTICAL READING 1

- Looking Good
- Food and Nutrition
- Working for a Living
- Managing Your Money

READING in context

READING
in context

PRACTICAL READING 1

PRACTICAL READING 2

READING NONFICTION 1

READING NONFICTION 2

READING FICTION 1

READING FICTION 2

SADDLEBACK
PUBLISHING·INC.

Three Watson
Irvine, CA 92618-2767

Website: www.sdlback.com

Development and Production: Laurel Associates, Inc.
Cover Design: Elisa Ligon
Interior Illustrations: Ginger Slonaker

ISBN 1-56254-189-7

Printed in the United States of America
09 08 07 06 05   9 8 7 6 5 4 3 2

CONTENTS

INTRODUCTION

A NOTE TO THE STUDENT

Skillful readers have many advantages in life. While they are in school, they obviously get better grades. But the benefits go far beyond the classroom. Good readers are also good thinkers, problem-solvers, and decision-makers. They can avoid many of the problems and frustrations that unskilled readers miss out on. In short, good readers have a much greater chance to be happy and successful in all areas of their lives.

READING IN CONTEXT is an all-around skill-building program. Its purpose is to help you achieve your goals in life by making you a better reader. Each of the six worktexts has been designed with your needs and interests in mind. The reading selections are engaging and informative—some lighthearted and humorous, others quite serious and thought-provoking. The follow-up exercises teach the essential skills and concepts that lead to reading mastery.

We suggest that you thumb through the book before you begin work. Read the table of contents. Notice that each of the four units is based on a unifying theme. Then take a moment to look through the four lessons that make up each theme-based unit. Scan one of the *Before reading* paragraphs that introduces a lesson. Glance at the *Preview* and *Review* pages that begin and end each unit. "Surveying" this book (or any book) in this informal way is called *prereading*. It helps you "get a fix on" the task ahead by showing you how the book is organized. Recognizing patterns is an important thinking skill in itself. And in this case it will make you more comfortable and confident as you begin your work.

Happy reading!

LOOKING GOOD

LESSON 1: Caring for Your Skin and Teeth
LESSON 2: Taking Care of Your Clothing
LESSON 3: Exercising for a Better Body
LESSON 4: Controlling Your Weight

When you complete the lessons in this unit, you will be able to answer questions like these:

- *What causes acne to appear in the teen years?*

- *How can bad breath be prevented?*

- *What kind of exercise uses **most** of your body's muscles?*

- *On a sensible reducing diet, how much weight can you expect to lose each week?*

PRETEST

Write **T** or **F** to show whether you think each statement is *true* or *false*.

1. _____ Plaque on your teeth can destroy your gum tissue.

2. _____ A pimple forms when bacteria invade a plugged pore.

3. _____ A grease stain on clothing can be removed with hydrogen peroxide.

4. _____ A good chemical stain remover can get rid of any kind of stain.

5. _____ The best time to work out is just before breakfast or dinner.

6. _____ A calorie is a measurement of the energy a food supplies to the body.

Pretest answers: 1. T 2. T 3. F 4. F 5. T 6. T

CARING FOR YOUR SKIN AND TEETH

Before reading . . .

Healthy skin and teeth are very important to good looks. The information in this lesson can teach you how to safeguard your clear complexion and your dazzling smile!

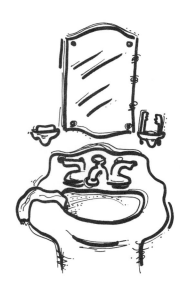

During the teen years, sex hormones bring about a great number of changes in the body. These changes affect the skin. Glands in the skin begin to produce more oil. Your face, neck, shoulders, and back may break out in pimples, or acne. Your hair may get oily, too.

This overflow of oil acts like a paste. It moves up to the surface of your skin and plugs up your pores. A whitehead is the tip of the plug. It stays white if air cannot reach it. When air does reach the plug, a chemical change takes place. The plug turns dark. Then it becomes a blackhead. Infection starts when bacteria get under one of these plugs. This is what causes a pimple.

For many teenagers, acne is a part of growing up. In adulthood, the pituitary gland settles down these hormones, and the acne will go away. In the meantime, follow these tips:

- Wash your face with a mild soap and water every day. This helps unclog your pores and kills bacteria.

- Stay away from greasy, fried, and sweet foods. They can make acne problems worse.

- Keep your fingers away from your face. Squeezing pimples can cause further infection and lasting scars.

- Get plenty of rest and eat fresh, natural foods. Stress and a poor diet can cause your skin to break out.

- If you have a bad case of acne, see a dermatologist. (A dermatologist is a doctor who specializes in skin problems.)

- Wash your hair daily. If your hair is very oily, you might try wearing a shorter hairstyle to keep your hair away from your face.

A great smile begins with healthy teeth. Unfortunately, the mouth is an ideal place for bacteria to grow. If sugar or bits of food stay in your mouth, bacteria will form a sticky covering called *plaque*. Over time, this plaque builds up on your teeth and can destroy your gum tissue. Left untreated, the plaque will attack the bone that holds your teeth in place. In the worst cases, plaque can cause the teeth to fall out.

Plaque cannot be removed just by brushing. Only a dentist can remove all of it by using special tools. But brushing regularly and using dental floss once a day can help remove a lot of the plaque.

Cavities are formed when acid made by bacteria eats away at the outer covering of your teeth. This outer covering is called *enamel*. When the acid eats into your inner tooth, called *dentin*, you may get a toothache. If the cavity reaches the pulp, the inner layer of the tooth, you may have to have the tooth pulled out. See your dentist right away if you have a toothache. Most small cavities are fairly easy for a dentist to repair.

Follow these simple guidelines to keep your teeth healthy:

- Brush after eating, especially after you eat something sweet.

- Use dental floss at least once a day.

- Visit the dentist twice a year.

- Remember: All foods can cause plaque!

DO YOU WORRY ABOUT HAVING BAD BREATH?

Bad breath is sometimes called *halitosis*. In healthy young people, bad breath is usually caused by bacteria's effect on food that gets stuck between the teeth. After eating, use dental floss to make sure that your mouth is food-free!

COMPREHENSION

Look back through the reading selection if you need help answering the questions.

1. What four areas of the body are often affected by acne?

   _____

2. What microscopic organisms can infect your teeth and skin?

   _____

3. What happens when air reaches a plugged pore?

   _____

4. What job can floss do better than a toothbrush can?

   _____

5. What common practice can leave you with lasting acne scars?

   _____

6. What is halitosis?

   _____

7. The reading selections on skin and dental care both suggest
   the same main idea. What is it?

   _____

SPELLING

Find the misspelled word in each sentence. Rewrite the word correctly on the line.

1. An excess of oil can clog your skin pours.   _____

2. Bits of food stuck in your teeth can cause
   bad breathe.   _____

3. A dermatologist specializes in skin problems.   _____

SUFFIXES

Complete each **boldface** word with the correct *suffix.*

1. **Unfortunat**_____, the mouth is an ideal place for bacteria
   to grow.

2. Remove plaque by brushing **regular**_____ and using
   dental floss.

3. Most **cavit**_____ are easy for a dentist to repair.

4. Plaque forms a sticky **cover**_____ on the teeth.

5. **Infect**_____ can start when oil plugs up a pore.

6. For many teens, acne is part of **grow**_____ up.

COMPOUND WORDS

Use words from the box to complete the *compound words* in the sentences.
Hint: You will *not* use all the words in the box.

brush	hood	flow	white	tooth
some	out	can	guide	teen
times	mean	in	black	every

1. Skin glands **some**_____ produce an **over**_____
   of oil.

2. When air reaches an oil plug, the plug becomes a
   _____**head**.

3. If acid eats _____**to** the dentin, you may get a
   _____**ache**.

4. A worn-out **tooth**_____ will not clean your
   teeth very well.

5. After eating _____**thing** sweet, be sure to brush
   your teeth.

6. Follow four simple _____**lines** to help keep your
   teeth healthy.

7. All the plaque on your teeth _____**not** be removed by brushing.

8. Most _____**age** acne goes away in **adult**_____; in the _____**time**, keep your skin clean!

PUZZLER

Use the clues to help you solve the crossword puzzle.

ACROSS

3. the hard outer coating of the teeth

5. a hole in a tooth caused by decay

6. body parts that produce necessary substances

8. produced by glands

DOWN

1. tiny, one-celled living things that can cause decay

2. strong thread used to clean between teeth

4. common skin disease caused by clogged oil glands

7. the largest of the body's organs; its outer covering

WORD COMPLETION

Add vowels (*a, e, i, o, u*) to complete the words in this important warning.

C__V__T__ __S   SH__ __LD   B__   TR__ __T__D

B__F__R__   TH__Y   D__   L__ST__NG   D__M__G__

T__   Y__ __R   T__ __TH!

DIAGRAM LABELS

Unscramble the words. Then use the unscrambled words to label the diagram correctly.

NITNED _____

MEANEL _____

LUPP _____

TIVCAY _____

1. _____

2. _____

3. _____

4. _____

SYNONYMS AND ANTONYMS

Look in the box for a word with the same or the opposite meaning of the **boldface** word in each phrase. Write the *synonym* or *antonym* on the line. Hint: You will *not* use all the words in the box.

physician	harsh	pinch	fresh	artificial
excessive	ample	destroy	shampoo	diseased

1. to **kill** bacteria

   SYNONYM: _____

2. **natural** foods

   ANTONYM: _____

3. **wash** your hair

   SYNONYM: _____

4. see a **doctor**

   SYNONYM: _____

5. **healthy** skin

   ANTONYM: _____

6. **plenty of** rest

   SYNONYM: _____

7. a **mild** soap

   ANTONYM: _____

8. **squeeze** pimples

   SYNONYM: _____

TAKING CARE OF YOUR CLOTHING

Before reading . . .

Good clothes are expensive. You want them to look good for a long time. The information in this lesson can help you take better care of your clothes. Read on to find out how to remove common stains, avoid wrinkles, and iron your clothes like an expert!

HOW TO REMOVE SPOTS

STAIN	WASHABLES
BLOOD	When fresh, sponge with cool water; rinse clear. If stain persists or has dried, sponge with diluted hydrogen peroxide; rinse.
CANDLE WAX	Freeze until wax is frozen. Brush off with wire brush. Pour boiling water through garment to melt and remove residue.
CHEWING GUM	Dab with ice to harden; scrape away as much as possible. Place between white blotters and press with warm iron, changing blotters as needed. Finish with cleaning fluid.
COFFEE OR TEA	Rinse in warm water; pour boiling water through; wash with soap. Treat traces with sodium percarbonate or sunlight.
FRUIT JUICES	Rinse immediately with cool water. Although dry fruit stains are difficult, try a warm borax solution soak or paste of cream tartar and warm water. After a half-hour, rinse.
GREASE (Butter, oil, etc.)	If fabric is washable, wash in warm, sudsy water. If not, sponge with solvent specifically formulated for grease.
INK	Saturate with alcohol-based hairspray; place an absorbent towel under stain; blot with rag. Repeat and launder as usual.
LIPSTICK, MAKEUP	Try towelettes on contact; launder normally. If stain remains, sponge with methylated spirits or household ammonia.
RED WINE	On sturdy fabric, cover stain with salt; pour just-boiled water through stain. Otherwise, blot, wash cold, dry. If that fails, try oil solvent followed by vinegar for remaining color.

SPEEDY SPOT REMOVAL

- Treat a stain as soon as possible. If you can, keep the garment moist until laundering it.

- Never rub a wet stain. If liquid is still in a ball on the surface, try to absorb it into the tip of a white cloth.

- Once a stain has dried, brush off what you can before attempting to use a chemical solvent.

- Always test cleaning agents first on a hidden seam or hem.

- Place fabric stain-side down on a paper towel or white cloth. Dab stain remover to the underside of the fabric, forcing the stain through and onto a towel or cloth.

- When in doubt, don't do anything! Consult a dry cleaner.

WRINKLE REMOVAL

- Metallic ironing board covers wick away needed steam. Use cotton covers.

- Don't press down hard on the iron—it's the heat and steam that smooth away wrinkles.

- Wet pants hung by the legs (not the waist) will dry with fewer wrinkles.

- Clothes that are slightly moist all over are easiest to iron (with a dry setting). When possible, remove clothes from dryer while damp and press immediately.

- Ironing in a circular motion can stretch out fabric. The best pressing motion is back and forth with the grain.

HOW TO IRON PANTS WITH POCKETS

1. *Waistband:* First, rotating top of pants, press the inside of waistband.

2. *Pockets:* Pull pockets inside out and press. Iron the rest of the pants around the pockets before pushing them back in place. Touch up the outside of the front and back.

3. *Legs:* Lay pants on board with seams aligned. Fold back the top leg; iron inside bottom leg. Flip pants over and repeat on other side. Then iron outside of top leg, using a burst of steam to set the creases; flip over and repeat.

HOW TO IRON A SHIRT WITH LONG SLEEVES

1. *Collar:* Press the inside of the collar, smoothing as you go to avoid puckers.

2. *Cuffs:* Press inside of unbuttoned cuffs.

3. *Sleeves:* Iron the cuff opening side first, then the opposite side. Hold sleeve flat to board to make sharp creases. Now iron outside cuffs.

4. *Body:* Iron the insides of yoke and back and then the outsides. Next, iron outside shirt fronts, moving the iron around the buttons. Iron outside of collar.

COMPREHENSION

Write **T** if the statement is *true* and **F** if the statement is *false*. Write **NI** for *no information* if the reading does not provide that information.

1. _____ To remove an ink stain, rinse the fabric in warm water.

2. _____ Before washing, pat a wet stain with a dry white cloth.

3. _____ Pressing the collar is the last step in ironing a shirt.

4. _____ Slightly damp clothes are easier to iron than dry clothes.

5. _____ Always iron the creases in both pant legs at the same time.

6. _____ Remember to iron the sleeve of a shirt inside out.

COMPOUND WORDS

Complete each sentence below with a compound word (one word made of two) from the reading.

1. Exposure to _____ may remove a slight coffee stain.

2. Rotate the top of the pants as you press the _____.

3. Dab stain remover on the _____ of the fabric.

4. To remove _____ and _____ stains, first try towelettes on contact.

READING A CHART

Draw a line to match each kind of stain with the appropriate stain remover.

1. **red wine**   a. ammonia

2. **ink**   b. peroxide

3. **lipstick**   c. salt

4. **blood**   d. hairspray

ANTONYMS

Unscramble the words from the reading. Then write each unscrambled word below the phrase that contains its *antonym* (word that means the opposite) in **boldface**.

SYSUD _____	**TEDULID** _____
ROBBAS _____	**SOOPTIPE** _____
SNIRE _____	**VEEMOR** _____

1. the **same** side

   _____

2. warm, **clear** water

   _____

3. **apply** product

   _____

4. **full-strength** peroxide

   _____

5. **lather** immediately

   _____

6. **repel** the stain

   _____

PUZZLER

Solve the crossword puzzle. The puzzle clues are *synonyms* (words with the same meaning) of words in the reading.

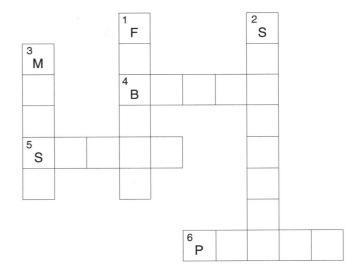

ACROSS

4. spray
5. spot
6. iron

DOWN

1. cloth
2. soak
3. damp

INFERENCE

Answer the questions in complete sentences.

1. Why do you think the article says to first test a cleaning agent on a "hidden" seam or hem?

   _____

2. Why should you consult a dry cleaner if you're in doubt about how to clean something?

_____

3. The article says that a metallic ironing board cover can wick away needed steam. What do you think "wick away" means?

_____

4. Why is it so important to try to remove a stain immediately?

_____

SPELLING

Circle the correctly spelled word in each group of words.

1. solvant   solvent   sollvint
2. chemical   chemicle   chemacll
3. resadue   resudue   residue

4. creeses   creases   creaces
5. seams   seems   seames
6. collar   coller   collor

LOOK IT UP!

Look in the dictionary for the definition of each **boldface** word. Write the definition on the line.

1. A paste made of cream of **tartar** and warm water can be used to remove fruit juice stains.

_____

_____

2. The best ironing motion is back and forth with the **grain** of the fabric.

_____

3. Sponge makeup stains with household **ammonia**

_____

4. When ironing a shirt, press the insides of the **yoke** and back before pressing the outsides.

_____

FORMS OF A WORD

In each sentence below you will find one word in the wrong form. First underline the incorrect word. Then write the correct *form* of the word on the line after each statement.

1. If a stain persist, sponge with hydrogen peroxide. _____

2. Freeze a spot of candle wax until the wax is froze. _____

3. Press with a warm iron, changed blotters as needed. _____

4. Pour boil water through the stain. _____

5. Sponge non-washable fabric with solvent specific formulated for grease. _____

6. Try oil solvent followed by vinegar to remove any remain traces of color. _____

7. Repeat the stain treatment and laundry as usual. _____

8. Never rubbing a wet stain. _____

DRAWING CONCLUSIONS

What reasonable conclusion can be drawn from the **boldface** word or words? Circle a letter to show your answer.

1. **When in doubt, don't do anything!**

   a. The stain has become permanent.

   b. The dry cleaner can remove any spot.

   c. You may destroy a garment by trying to clean it.

2. **Wet pants hung by the legs dry with fewer wrinkles.**

   a. Hanging wet pants by the cuffs saves ironing.

   b. On a clothesline, hang pants from the waist.

   c. Clothes dryers always put wrinkles in pant legs.

EXERCISING FOR A BETTER BODY

Before reading . . .

Bodybuilders aren't necessarily any healthier than anybody else. But *every* body—including yours—needs some kind of regular exercise to function at its best. This lesson presents basic information about "moving your muscles" for good health and good looks.

LIGHT EXERCISE

walking
bowling
working on a car
doing housework
baseball

MODERATE EXERCISE

flag football
skating
skiing
tennis
golf

STRENUOUS EXERCISE

running
swimming
basketball
gymnastics
shoveling snow

One of the goals of any exercise program should be to put unused muscles to work. It should also get your heart working to its fullest. Your exercise program should be fun, and you should be comfortable doing it regularly. There are many ways to reach these goals.

People exercise for different reasons. Some people work out to become strong. Others exercise to lose weight, to improve their appearance, or just to relax. Some people exercise simply because it's fun and it's good for their bodies. Thinking about *why* you want to exercise will help you choose the program that is right for you.

First think about your normal activities. Do you spend most of the day sitting at a desk? If so, many of your muscles are probably not as strong as they should be. Swimming, which uses most of the muscles in the body, is an excellent way to put them to work. Swimming is very good for your heart and lungs, too.

Tennis, running, bicycling, and skating also strengthen your muscles. All these activities burn several hundred calories an hour.

If you're on your feet all day or doing physical labor, calisthenics and bowling are good exercises for you. They burn fewer calories and use fewer muscles than exercises such as swimming or running. Calisthenics and bowling are also good activities for people who want to exercise mainly to relax and to enjoy themselves.

Most neighborhood community centers offer exercise, dance, and swim classes. These regular workouts help you get in shape and meet other people who share your goals.

Many people enjoy walking to school and work or hiking the trails in parks. Walking is a good way to prepare yourself for the day and to relax afterward. Instead of taking an elevator all the time, why not walk up and down the stairs? Climbing a few flights is good for your heart and muscles—and it burns calories, too!

You'll see and feel the greatest results if you exercise for 30 to 60 minutes several times a week. This is better for you than working out for several hours on one day. Many people find that a varied program works best. You might walk to school or work, swim twice a week, and play basketball on weekends. Or you could run three mornings a week and bowl on the weekends. As long as your personal exercise routine is followed regularly, it will help you live a longer, healthier life.

> ### EXERCISE DOS AND DON'TS
>
> - Start out slowly. Don't push yourself too hard. With time, you'll be able to exercise longer and you'll be better at the exercises you do.
>
> - Never exercise just after eating. Wait at least an hour. The best time to work out is right before breakfast or dinner.
>
> - Do warm-up exercises such as stretching and bending before beginning any more strenuous activities.
>
> - Don't give up! It may take some time— perhaps months—to see the results.
>
> - Make an effort to get some form of exercise—walking, stretching and bending, or climbing stairs— every day. Make it a habit.

COMPREHENSION

Write **T** if the statement is *true* and **F** if the statement is *false*. Write **NI** for *no information* if the article does not provide that information.

1. _____ Exercise is more important for overweight people than for underweight people.

2. _____ A sport such as bowling provides light exercise.

3. _____ Children require more exercise than adults do.

4. _____ People who do physical labor all day need less recreational exercise than people who work at a desk.

5. _____ "No pain, no gain" is a good guideline for how long you should work out.

6. _____ Activities like skating and bicycling burn several thousand calories an hour.

7. _____ Swimming works out most of the muscles in your body.

8. _____ Square dancing gives your muscles more exercise than ballroom dancing.

9. _____ The best time to exercise is immediately after eating.

10. _____ A regular program of exercise will help you live longer.

PUZZLER

Use the clues to help you complete the crossword puzzle.

ACROSS

2. units measuring energy that food supplies to the body

6. neither too much nor too little

7. the large muscle in the chest that pumps blood

8. to rest; take it easy

DOWN

1. an aim or purpose

3. drawing out body parts to their full length

4. behavior repeated so often it becomes automatic

5. a regular routine

6. body tissue that stretches or squeezes to move parts of the body

SYLLABLES

Divide the following words into syllables (the separate sounds in a word.)

1. community   2. results   3. moderate

_____/_____/_____/_____   _____/_____   _____/_____/_____

COMPOUND WORDS

Write a *compound word* to complete each sentence. Choose the first part of the compound from List A and the second part from List B.

LIST A			LIST B		
them	some		self	selves	
body	break		hood	fast	
work	your		out	ends	
week	neighbor		times	builders	

1. Most _____ community centers offer exercise classes.

2. _____ aren't necessarily healthier than anybody else.

3. Don't push _____ too hard.

4. A good time to exercise is right before _____.

5. Do one exercise during the week, and a different exercise on

_____.

6. _____ it takes weeks or months to see dramatic results.

7. Many people exercise just to relax and enjoy _____.

8. Stretch and bend before you begin a strenuous _____.

SYNONYMS

The scrambled words are *synonyms* (words that mean the same) of the **boldface** words in the sentences. First unscramble the words in the box. Then write each word next to its synonym.

SCEELT _____	**NIGRID** _____
OKSOL _____	**HAREC** _____
SULAU _____	**DIPSNELD** _____

1. Regular exercise improves your **appearance** _____.

2. Thinking about your exercise goals will help you **choose** _____ the program that is right for you.

3. What are your **normal** _____ daily activities?

4. Swimming is an **excellent** _____ way to put your muscles to work.

5. Walk up and down stairs instead of **taking** _____ the elevator.

6. There are many ways to **achieve** _____ your goals.

VOCABULARY

Write a letter to match each term with its definition.

1. _____ **strenuous**   a. individual; not having to do with others

2. _____ **capacity**   b. a regular way of doing something

3. _____ **routine**   c. simple gymnastic exercises

4. _____ **personal**   d. needing a lot of energy and effort

5. _____ **calisthenics**   e. maximum ability to function

EXAMPLES

Circle two examples of each **boldface** word or phrase.

1. **light exercise**

   shoveling snow   digging ditches   walking   doing housework

2. **calisthenics**

   push-ups   bungee jumping   jumping jacks   gymnastics

3. **activities**

   calories   sitting   weekends   stretching

4. **goals**

   weight loss   preparation   dance class   relaxation

WORD FORMS

Write the *form* of the **boldface** word that correctly completes each sentence.

1. If you do a **(varied)** _____ of different exercises, you won't become bored.

2. Your exercise program should be **(comfort)** _____ and fun.

3. Regular exercise will help you live a longer, **(health)** _____ life.

4. You might **(variation)** _____ your workout from one day to the next.

5. Good **(healthy)** _____ is an important part of a happy life.

6. Remember to dress **(comforting)** _____ for your workout!

CONTROLLING YOUR WEIGHT

Before reading . . .

Careless eating habits cause many people to become overweight. To look and feel your best, avoid eating too many high-calorie foods. Think about your age, height, and body frame. These factors determine the number of calories your body needs. In general, however, teenage boys need about 2,700 calories a day and teenage girls need about 2,300.

There is no magic pill or program for losing weight quickly. The best reducing diets give you all the energy and nutrients you need to stay strong and healthy. If you lose weight slowly—the healthy way— you will feel good and keep the weight off. That's a promise that so-called "miracle" diet products can't make!

Weight loss may not be easy, but the process itself is simple. If your body burns off more calories than it takes in, you will lose weight. If the number of calories you take in each day equals the energy your body burns, your weight will stay the same.

Some people worry *too much* about losing weight. These people can develop life-threatening eating disorders called anorexia and bulimia. That's why it's a good idea to see a doctor before starting a diet. A doctor can tell you how much weight you need to lose and help you reach your goal.

The chart below shows the calories contained in some common foods. Think about the foods you usually eat. Are you doing enough daily exercise to burn off all those calories?

FOOD	*CALORIES
MILK PRODUCTS	
Milk	
skim .... 1 cup 90	
whole .... 1 cup 160	
Yogurt .... 1 cup 160	
Cheese	
cheddar .... 1¼" cube 115	
American ..... 1¼" cube 115	
Swiss .... 1¼" cube 115	
cottage .... ½ cup 120	
Ice cream .... ½ cup 130	
Cream .... ¼ cup 80	
VEGETABLES	
Broccoli .... ½ cup, cooked .. 20	
Carrots .... ½ cup, cooked or raw 30	
Celery .... ½ cup, raw 10	
Potato 1 85	
Squash .... ¼ cup, cooked .. 15	

FOOD	*CALORIES
FRUITS	
Apple 1 80	
Banana 1 100	
Blueberries .... ½ cup 40	
Cantaloupe .... ¼ melon 40	
Grapes .... ½ cup 60	
Orange 1 65	
Peach 1 40	
Pear 1 100	
Raisins .... ½ cup 120	
MEAT, POULTRY, AND EGGS	
Beef, lamb, and veal 3 ounces, cooked ... 180–225	
Chicken 1 drumstick and thigh, fried .. 250	
Turkey ..... 3 ounces, no skin 180	
Hamburger .. 3 ounces, cooked .. 250	
Hot dog 1 160	
Eggs .... 1 large 80	

FOOD	*CALORIES
CEREALS, BREADS, AND SPAGHETTI	
Bread, toast ... 1 slice 70	
Oatmeal .... 1 cup, cooked .. 110	
Ready-to-eat cereal .... 1 ounce 100	
Hamburger roll .... 1 medium 120	
Spaghetti, 1 cup, rice .... cooked 200	

* A calorie is a unit for measuring the amount of energy a food supplies to the body.

TIPS FOR LOSING WEIGHT EFFECTIVELY

- Set a realistic goal. Don't try to lose too much weight too fast. Work toward the goal suggested by your doctor.

- To lose weight, you will have to cut out some high-calorie foods. But don't cut out *all* your favorites, or you will feel deprived.

- Exercise. Swimming, running, and playing sports all burn up unwanted calories and reduce stress.

- Don't get discouraged. You won't lose weight every day. On a healthy low-calorie diet, you can expect to lose two to three pounds a week. (That's about 25 pounds in only six months!)

- Eat three meals every day. If you want to lose weight, skipping meals is not the way to do it.

- Eat lots of low-calorie foods such as fresh fruits and vegetables as snacks. You won't feel hungry, and these foods are good for you.

- Develop some new interests that don't involve food. Join a club, for example, or learn how to play a new sport.

- Don't "wolf" your food. Eat slowly. Chew your food well. You'll be less likely to eat too much, and you'll also feel more relaxed.

- Drink eight glasses of water every day. Water reduces your appetite and washes excess fat out of your body.

- Reward yourself for your good work. Go to a movie with a friend, or buy yourself a treat other than food. Do something you really enjoy doing.

- Be patient! Longtime eating habits are hard to break. New habits are developed the same way the old ones were—by repetition. The longer you stick to a sensible diet, the more "normal" it will feel to eat that way.

LOOKING GOOD

- Stand and sit straight. You can add to your height and lose two inches off your waist by standing tall.

- Wear clothing that is flattering to your body frame. A large person, for example, can wear dark colors or stripes that go up and down. This makes the body appear taller and thinner.

- Smile! A cheerful manner and a positive attitude add a lot to an attractive appearance.

COMPREHENSION

Write **T** or **F** to show whether the statement is *true* or *false*. Write **NI** if there is *no information* in the reading to help you decide.

1. _____ Some thin people mistakenly believe they need to lose weight.

2. _____ Most overweight people eat whole pies and cakes for dessert.

3. _____ Some very expensive diet plans can make you lose 10 pounds overnight.

4. _____ More teenage girls are overweight than teenage boys.

5. _____ The human body burns calories to create energy.

6. _____ People who are only 10 or 15 pounds overweight look better than extremely skinny people.

7. _____ Losing weight very quickly is the best way to make sure the weight stays off.

8. _____ Most teenage girls need to take in about 2,300 calories a day.

VOCABULARY

Circle a letter to show the meaning of the **boldface** word.

1. What **factors** determine how many calories your body needs?

    a. fruits, vegetables, cereals   b. age, height, body frame   c. friends, parents, doctor

2. **Active** people burn off more calories than inactive people.

    a. people who walk, lift, bend, stretch, exercise   b. people who plan activities   c. people who need little sleep

3. **Reduce** the number of high-calorie foods in your diet.

    a. eliminate   b. water down   c. lessen

PUZZLER

Use the clues to help you solve the crossword puzzle.
Answers are words that complete the sentences.

ACROSS

3. The average American woman weights 134 ___.

5. Habits are learned by constant ___.

7. ___ is a life-threatening eating disorder.

8. Make sure that your weight-loss goal is ___.

DOWN

1. A ___ is a unit for measuring the energy in food.

2. Drinking lots of water can help to control your ___.

4. The more you exercise, the more ___ your body burns.

6. There is no magic way to lose ___ quickly.

SUFFIXES

Rewrite the **boldface** words to correctly complete each sentence. The new words you write will end with a suffix from the box.

ly	ing	ible	less	tion

1. Stripes that go up and down are **(flatter)** _____ on a large person.

2. **(Care)** _____ eating habits cause people to gain weight.

3. Think about the foods you **(usual)** _____ eat.

4. If you eat a **(sense)** _____ diet, you will lose
   weight slowly.

5. **(Skip)** _____ meals is not a good way to lose weight.

6. Eat several **(day)** _____ servings of fruit and vegetables.

7. Healthy new eating habits are learned by **(repeat)** _____.

SYLLABLES

Divide the words in the box into *syllables* (the separate sounds in a word).

calorie	energy	bulimia	realistic
hamburger	determine	repetition	effectively

_____/_____/_____   _____/_____/_____/_____

_____/_____/_____   _____/_____/_____/_____

_____/_____/_____   _____/_____/_____/_____

_____/_____/_____   _____/_____/_____/_____

READING A CHART

1. Which vegetable listed on the chart has
   the lowest number of calories?   _____

2. Which three servings of fruit contain the same number of calories?

   _____ _____ _____

3. How many calories are in a hamburger
   and a hamburger bun?   _____

4. How much ice cream is considered to be one serving? _____

28

5. How many calories are in two slices of toast? _____

6. Which vegetable listed in the chart has
   the most calories?   _____

7. If you have a hot dog and an orange for lunch, how
   many calories will you consume?   _____

8. If you melt two cubes of cheddar cheese in two
   scrambled eggs, how many calories will you consume? _____

9. One cup of whole milk has how many more calories
   than one cup of skim milk?   _____

ANTONYMS

Circle the *antonym* (word that means the opposite) of each **boldface** word.

1. Exercise helps to reduce **stress**. (nervousness / relaxation / worry)

2. A **sensible** diet works slowly. (ridiculous / knowledgeable / prudent)

3. A **cheerful** manner is very attractive. (hilarious / polite / grumpy)

4. **Reward** yourself for your own good work. (treat / punish / applaud)

SENTENCE COMPLETION

Unscramble the words to complete the sentences.

1. There is no such thing as a **CLEARIM** _____ diet.

2. There are 160 calories in a cup of **RUGTOY** _____.

3. Standing straight adds to your **THIGHE** _____.

4. New **TIBASH** _____ are formed by repeating
   new behaviors.

5. Fresh **SUFTIR** _____ make healthy snacks.

REVIEW

VOCABULARY

Unscramble the words to complete the sentences.

1. Dental floss can help remove the **QUELPA** _____
   on your teeth.

2. Brush off a dried stain before using a cleaning **VOLNETS**
   _____.

3. Warm up slowly before doing **RENTSUOSU** _____
   exercise.

4. A single serving of food weighs just a few **ECUNOS**
   _____.

MULTIPLE CHOICE

Circle a letter to answer each question.

1. What can regular stair climbing do for your health?
   a. strengthen your heart   c. burn off calories
   b. relax your muscles   d. both a and c

2. What determines the number of calories your body needs?
   a. your goals, hopes,   c. the fact that you
      and dreams   have a sweet tooth
   b. your age, height,   d. charts of the calorie
      and body frame   content of various foods

3. When pressing a pair of pants, what is the last part to be ironed?
   a. collar   b. pockets   c. waistband   d. legs

4. Squeezing pimples can have which two bad effects?
   a. infection and scarring   c. clogged pores and redness
   b. more oil and smoother skin   d. dry skin with oily patches

FOOD AND NUTRITION

LESSON 1: The Four Food Groups
LESSON 2: Vitamins and Minerals
LESSON 3: Buying Groceries
LESSON 4: Vegetarianism

When you complete the lessons in this unit, you will be able to answer questions like these:

■ *Why do teenagers need to eat more dairy foods than adults do?*

■ *Do most people need to supplement their diet with vitamin pills?*

■ *How do skillful shoppers compare grocery prices?*

■ *What foods does a **lactovegetarian** choose not to eat?*

PRETEST

Write **T** or **F** to show whether you think each statement is *true* or *false*.

1. _____ The four major food groups are the meat group, the vegetable group, the fruit group, and the milk group.

2. _____ To stay healthy, people need very large amounts of certain vitamins.

3. _____ You'll save money by planning your menus around foods that are on sale.

4. _____ Healthy meals are less expensive than junk foods.

5. _____ Teenagers need six daily servings from the bread and cereals group.

6. _____ A mixture of beans and rice provides more protein than either food eaten alone.

Pretest answers: 1. F   2. F   3. T   4. T   5. F   6. T

THE FOUR FOOD GROUPS

Before reading . . .

Are there certain foods you can't get enough of and other foods you never eat? Healthy nutrition requires a *variety* of foods. In this lesson, you will learn something about the major food groups that should be an everyday part of your regular diet.

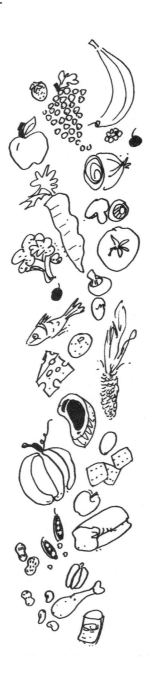

A well-balanced diet includes daily servings from the four food groups: the fruits and vegetables group, the milk group, the meat group, and the bread and cereal group.

It's important to eat the right amount of food from each food category every day. If you do, you'll get all the nutrients you need to grow and to stay healthy. You'll have a varied and interesting diet, too.

The *milk group* includes whole, skim, and low-fat milk. It also includes products made from milk—such as ice cream, yogurt, and cheese. These foods give you calcium, which helps keep your bones and teeth strong. One cup of milk or yogurt counts as one serving. So do two cups of cottage cheese or one and a half cups of ice cream. Teenagers need four servings from the milk group every day. Adults need two.

All fresh and canned fruits and fruit juices are in the *fruits and vegetables group*. So are all vegetables—such as broccoli, cauliflower, lettuce, and spinach. These foods are good sources of important vitamins. Even a small vitamin deficiency can make you tired and nervous. Fresh fruits and vegetables are best. One small vegetable or fruit counts as one serving. So does half a cup of cooked vegetables or one cup of fruit juice. Try to eat four servings from the fruits and vegetables group every day.

The *meat group* includes all meats, such as beef, chicken, pork, lamb, and veal. It also includes eggs, poultry, fish, dried beans, peas, and peanut butter. All of the foods in this group give you protein, iron, fat, and vitamins, which are necessary for life. Try to eat at least two servings from this group every day. Two eggs or two to three ounces of meat, poultry, or fish count as one serving. So does one cup of cooked dried beans or four tablespoons of peanut butter.

The fourth group is the *bread and cereal group*. The foods in this group provide vitamins, minerals, and carbohydrates. (Carbohydrates give you energy.) All breads and cereals, including muffins and rolls, are in this group. Rice, macaroni and spaghetti, popcorn, crackers, potatoes, and corn are also included. You need at least four servings from this group every day. Try to include at least one serving with every meal. A roll or one slice of bread is one serving. One half to three quarters of a cup of rice or macaroni is also one serving.

Many people try to eat nourishing foods at meals, but they snack on anything that's around. They end up eating junk food instead of healthy foods. Junk foods have a lot of sugar, fat, and salt. They contain few nutrients.

What snacks do you usually eat? The next time you reach for junk food, think about what you're eating. Maybe one of these healthy snacks would taste just as good or even better:

- Cheese and crackers
- Celery with peanut butter
- Popcorn without butter
- Fruit
- Nuts
- Carrot sticks

MILK GROUP

Adults need 2 servings every day.

Teens need 4 servings.

One serving is:

1 cup milk or yogurt
2 cups cottage cheese
2 ounces of cheese
1½ cups ice cream

VEGETABLE-FRUIT GROUP

Adults and teens need 4 servings every day.

One serving is:

1 orange or apple
½ cup small salad
½ grapefruit
½ cup vegetables

MEAT GROUP

Adults and teens need 2 servings every day.

One serving is:

2 eggs
4 tablespoons peanut butter
3 ounces meat, fish, or poultry

BREAD-CEREAL GROUP

Adults and teens need 4 servings every day.

One serving is:

1 slice of bread
½ to ¾ cup cooked cereal
½ to ¾ cup cooked rice or macaroni

COMPREHENSION

1. Name the four food groups represented in a healthy diet.

   _____

2. Foods in which group provide carbohydrates? _____

3. What important mineral is provided
   by foods in the milk group?   _____

4. How many servings of bread and cereal
   does a person need every day?   _____

5. Two cups of yogurt count as how many servings? _____

6. What do carbohydrates do for your body? _____

DRAWING CONCLUSIONS

Write **T** or **F** to show whether each statement is *true* or *false*.

1. _____ The word diet is only used to describe a weight-loss
   program.

2. _____ Some foods are more nutritious than others.

3. _____ Strict vegetarians might have trouble getting enough
   protein in their diets.

4. _____ If you eat enough meat, you don't have to eat as many
   fruits and vegetables.

SENTENCE COMPLETION

Unscramble the words from the reading to correctly complete the sentences.

1. Four tablespoons of **APEUNT TUBERT** _____
   count as one serving of meat.

34

2. **DROPSTUC** _____ made from milk include ice cream and cottage cheese.

3. One serving of **ACRAMNOI** _____ is about three quarters of a cup.

4. Teenagers need four **YALID** _____ servings of foods from the milk group.

PUZZLER

Use the clues to help you complete the crossword puzzle.

ACROSS

3. the small, starchy grains of a plant grown in a warm climate

5. edible plant part that contains the seeds inside a sweet, juicy pulp

7. a thick, soft food made from fermented milk

9. leafy green vegetable; Popeye's favorite

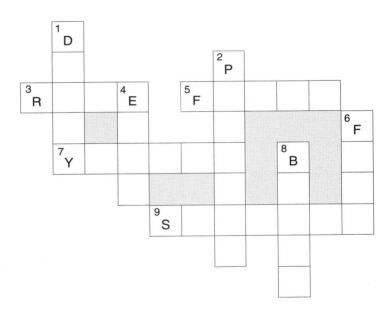

DOWN

1. describes products made from milk, such as butter and cheese

2. important substance in foods such as meat, eggs, cheese

4. laid by hens

6. water animals with fins, gills, and scales

8. edible seeds taken from plant pods

CATEGORIES

List the foods in the box under the correct headings.

custard	pretzels	liver	sardines
sauerkraut	cheddar	raisins	granola
milkshake	turkey	bacon	cream
cantaloupe	noodles	saltines	onions

MILK GROUP

_____

_____

_____

_____

FRUITS AND VEGETABLES

_____

_____

_____

_____

MEAT GROUP

_____

_____

_____

_____

BREAD AND CEREAL GROUP

_____

_____

_____

_____

SPELLING

Underline the misspelled word in each sentence. Then write the sentence correctly on the line.

1. One small vegtable or fruit counts as one serving.

   _____

2. A cup of cooked dryed beans gives you protein.

   _____

3. Brocolli is an excellent source of vitamins.

_____

4. The meat group includes poltry such as chicken and turkey.

_____

5. Potatos and corn give your body important carbohydrates.

_____

6. Cowliflower is a good source of essential vitamins.

_____

PARTS AND WHOLES

What food ingredients are contained in the following menu items? Write the names of two food groups after each item.

1. **pumpkin pie** _____ _____

2. **chicken noodle soup** _____ _____

3. **hot dog** _____ _____

4. **grilled cheese sandwich** _____ _____

5. **bean burrito** _____ _____

SYNONYMS

Draw a line to match each word on the left with its *synonym* (word with the same or nearly the same meaning) on the right.

1. **fresh**   a. fat-free

2. **nourishing**   b. processed

3. **canned**   c. wholesome

4. **skim**   d. raw

VITAMINS AND MINERALS

Before reading . . .

Have you ever heard of *beriberi*? About 120 years ago, this devastating disease crippled two-thirds of the Japanese navy. Then a discovery was made. Sailors who ate *whole* rice, hull and all, stayed disease-free. Only those who ate polished rice became sick. When the sailors' diet was changed, the disease disappeared. At the time, no one knew why. The vitamin B in the rice hulls had not yet been identified.

FACTS ABOUT MINERALS

- Minerals make up a large part of our bones and teeth.

- Smaller amounts of minerals are an essential part of our muscles, blood, and nerves.

In 1906, Frederick G. Hopkins, a professor at Cambridge University in England, discovered that certain factors in food were necessary for good health. He called those substances "accessory food factors." But it was a Polish scientist, Casimir Funk, who suggested the name *vitamine* (later changed to *vitamin*) which means "necessary to life." He was the first to isolate one of these substances. He called it vitamin B.

DAILY REQUIREMENTS OF MAJOR VITAMINS AND MINERALS

		MINERALS				VITAMINS				
	AGE	WEIGHT (lbs.)	CALCIUM (gm.)	IRON (mg.)	A (I.U.)	C (mg.)	D (I.U.)	THIAMINE (mg.)	RIBOFLAVIN (mg.)	NIACIN (mg.)
MEN										
Inactive	25	154	0.8	10	5,000	75		1.2	1.8	16
Active	25	154	0.8	10	5,000	75		1.6	1.8	21
Very Active	25	154	0.8	10	5,000	75		1.8	1.8	30
WOMEN										
Inactive	25	128	0.8	12	5,000	70		1.0	1.5	13
Active	25	128	0.8	12	5,000	70		1.2	1.5	17
Very Active	25	128	0.8	12	5,000	70		1.5	1.5	20
CHILDREN	1–3	27	1.0	7	2,000	35	400	0.7	1.0	8
	4–6	40	1.0	8	2,500	50	400	0.9	1.3	11
	7–9	60	1.0	10	3,500	60	400	1.1	1.5	14
	10–12	79	1.2	12	4,500	75	400	1.3	1.8	17
BOYS	13–15	108	1.4	15	5,000	90	400	1.6	2.1	21
	16–20	139	1.3	15	5,000	100	400	1.8	2.5	25
GIRLS	13–15	108	1.3	15	5,000	80	400	1.3	2.0	17
	16–20	120	1.3	15	5,000	80	400	1.2	1.9	16

lbs.=pound, gm.=gram, mg.=milligram, I.U.=International Units

Today it is well-known that vitamins are nutrients that regulate body processes. Human beings need only small amounts of vitamins to preserve health and well-being. At least a dozen vitamins are necessary to health, but experts have determined our *exact* needs for only six. These are vitamins A, C, D, and the B vitamins—thiamine, riboflavin, and niacin. Each of these vitamins performs a specific function and cannot be replaced by any other. The continuing lack of any one vitamin results in a deficiency disease, such as rickets, scurvy, or pellagra.

Read the chart to find out about the health benefits of some important vitamins.

VITAMIN	BODY BENEFIT	SOURCES
Vitamin A	growth	eggs, carrots, dark-green leafy vegetables, sardines, oysters
Vitamin B complex (B1, B2, B6, B12)	skin, appetite, calm nerves	chicken, tuna, beef, dry beans, whole-grain cereals
Vitamin C	gums, skin, bones, teeth, fighting infection	oranges, grapefruit, juices, limes, tomatoes, cabbage, red and green peppers, broccoli
Vitamin D	teeth and bones	milk, salmon, tuna, eggs, liver
Vitamin E	red blood cells, muscles	butter, eggs, liver, green vegetables, milk
Vitamin K	blood	tomatoes, eggs, liver, green leafy vegetables

The chart below lists some important minerals and tells how they keep you healthy.

MINERAL	BODY BENEFIT	SOURCES
Calcium	bones	milk, ice cream, lettuce, kale, mustard greens
Iron	builds hemoglobin in blood (helps red blood cells carry oxygen)	liver, eggs, dried fruit, leafy green vegetables
Iodine	hormones made by the thyroid gland	seafoods, salt with iodine
Copper	red blood cells, brain	nuts, raisins, mushrooms
Magnesium	bones and soft tissues	beef, corn, some cereals, leafy green vegetables
Zinc	growth and hormones	milk, eggs, seafoods, beef

COMPREHENSION

Answer the questions in complete sentences.

1. What two parts of the human body are largely made up
   of minerals?

   _____

2. What is the meaning of the word vitamin?

   _____

3. About how many different kinds of vitamins are required to
   maintain human health?

   _____

4. Do doctors think that most Americans need vitamin pills?

   _____

5. Milk, butter, and eggs are good sources of which vitamin?

   _____

6. Which mineral promotes growth and the development of hormones?

   _____

WORD COMPLETION

Add *vowels* (a, e, i, o, u) to complete the words.

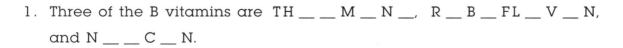

1. Three of the B vitamins are TH __ __ M __ N __, R __ B __ FL __ V __ N,
   and N __ __ C __ N.

2. Females require more __ R __ N in their diet than males do.

3. A person's daily requirement of C __ LC __ __ M is measured in grams.

4. T __ __ N __ G __ boys require more vitamin C than people in any other age group.

5. The abbreviation I.U. stands for a measurement called __ NT __ RN __ T __ __ N __ L __ N __ T __.

PUZZLER

Use the clues to help you solve the crossword puzzle.

ACROSS

2. fibers that connect body parts to the brain and spinal cord

4. lack of, or an insufficient amount of

7. food substances necessary for life and growth

8. red liquid that pumps through the body

DOWN

1. highest-ranking college or university teacher

3. natural substance in the earth that was never animal or vegetable

5. the usual group of foods eaten

6. outer covering of a seed or fruit

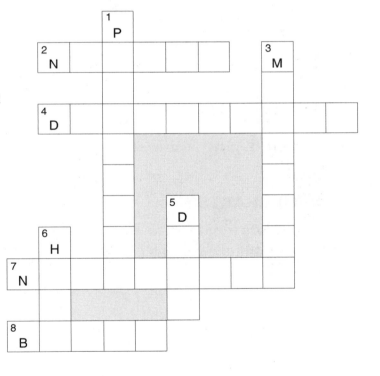

SYNONYMS AND ANTONYMS

Read the words in the box. Find a *synonym* (word that means the same) and an *antonym* (word that means the opposite) for the **boldface** word in each phrase. Write the synonyms and antonyms on the lines. Hint: You will *not* use all the words in the box.

entire	useless	destroy	deadly	necessary	sick
healthy	enhancing	peeled	natural	emerged	stale
vanished	multiplied	vitamin	mineral	maintain	acted

	SYNONYM	ANTONYM
1. sailors stayed **disease-free**	_____	_____
2. disease **disappeared**	_____	_____
3. to **preserve** health	_____	_____
4. **whole** rice	_____	_____
5. this **devastating** disease	_____	_____
6. **essential** part of muscles	_____	_____

READING CHARTS

Study the charts of vitamins and minerals. Find the information you need to answer the questions.

1. Name four specific seafoods that add vitamins to your diet.

   _____   _____

   _____   _____

2. Name two minerals that are partially supplied by seafood.

   _____   _____

3. Name one vitamin that benefits muscles. _____

4. Name one mineral needed by the brain. _____

5. Name three vitamins provided by liver.

   _____ _____ _____

6. Name two minerals provided by eggs.

   _____ _____

7. Name four vegetables that contain vitamin C.

   _____ _____

   _____ _____

PLURALS

Read each *singular* noun below. Write each noun in its *plural* form.

1. **substance** _____   4. **accessory** _____

2. **discovery** _____   5. **function** _____

3. **process** _____   6. **tooth** _____

NOTING DETAILS

1. Who was the first person to
   isolate and name a vitamin?   _____

2. What four diseases are caused by deficiency of a vitamin?

   _____ _____

   _____ _____

3. What was the first spelling
   of the word vitamin?   _____

4. Do very inactive adults need more of the B vitamins
   than active adults do?   _____

5. Do people who are still growing need more calcium
   than grown people do?   _____

BUYING GROCERIES

Before reading. . .

Most people shop for groceries once a week. Some people buy groceries every day. Are you a skillful shopper? Do you know how to buy the highest-quality foods at the lowest prices?

Before you go to the grocery store, spend a few minutes thinking about the week ahead. Begin your grocery list with any basic items—such as bread and milk—that you use every day. Then think about the meals you're planning to serve. Do you have all the ingredients in your cupboard or refrigerator? If not, write down the ingredients you need to buy.

Look at the grocery store ads in your local newspaper. Compare the prices of the same foods at two or more different markets. Make sure the stores are fairly close to your house. Remember that your time is worth money, too. You don't want to travel a long way just to save a few cents!

Be careful when you're comparing prices. Some products seem to be the same at first glance. But when you look closer, you'll see that the amount of food in the jar or can is not the same. A lower-priced jar of jelly, for example, may cost less because it weighs less.

To compare prices accurately, you need to figure out the price per ounce. You can do this by dividing the price by the number of ounces.

Reading grocery store ads can give you ideas for healthy, low-cost meals. Keep an eye out for sales. Maybe you were thinking about making

ARE SNACK FOODS A GOOD BUY?

Snack foods cost more per ounce than nearly all other food products. And most snack foods are very high in sugar, salt, and fats. Did you know you can buy *three* pounds of bananas for the same price as *one* bag of potato chips?

spaghetti for Sunday dinner, for example. Then you see an ad for pork roast at 50 percent off the usual price. To take advantage of the sale, you might decide to change your menu.

You can also compare the prices of different brands at the same store. Brand names can make a big difference in price. *Generic* foods have no brand name and no fancy packaging. These are the least expensive packaged foods— but you won't find them in all grocery stores.

The other two categories of brands are *nationally advertised brands* and *store brands*. Nationally advertised brands, of course, are the big-name brands you see advertised in newspapers, magazines, and on TV. Store brands are less expensive than nationally advertised brands. These brands are put out by a chain that includes many grocery stores.

Have you seen products displayed at the front of the store or at the end of the aisles? These displays are meant to catch your attention. Don't buy something just because it is attractively displayed. Think before you buy! Always ask yourself if the product is something you really need, and then compare prices.

COMPREHENSION

Circle a letter to show how each sentence should be completed.

1. The first items on your grocery list should be

   a. tasty snacks you've been craving.

   b. basic foods you eat every day.

   c. anything at all that's on sale.

2. In order to do comparison shopping, you must

   a. divide the price by the number of ounces.

   b. divide the number of ounces by the price.

   c. subtract the ounces from the price.

3. You can compare the prices of food items by

   a. shopping at two different stores.

   b. comparing different brands at one store.

   c. both a and b.

4. The best place to find grocery store ads is

   a. on television.

   b. in the newspaper.

   c. at the movies.

5. Foods that come in generic packages

   a. are more expensive than store-brand foods.

   b. are better quality than brand-name foods.

   c. are less expensive than brand-name foods.

6. Food items arranged in special displays are

   a. not a good choice if you don't need them.

   b. the best bargains in the store.

   c. priced higher than they should be.

7. You can save as much as 40 percent on your food bill by

   a. buying lots of snack foods.

   b. buying the least expensive brands.

   c. shopping only every other week.

WORD FORMS

Complete each sentence with the correct form of the **boldface** word.

1. We always go grocery **(shop)** _____ on Friday.

2. A skillful **(shop)** _____ always compares prices.

3. You make a **(compare)** _____ when you study the similarities of and differences between two products.

4. One who runs a food store is called a **(grocery)** _____.

5. Shopping wisely can save money and help you maintain your **(healthy)** _____.

6. You might **(decision)** _____ to change your menu if you find a good sale on something else.

PUZZLER

Use the clues to help you solve the crossword puzzle. Answers are words that complete the sentences.

ACROSS

2. A ___ is a number of stores owned by one company.

5. All foods sold by a store are called ___.

7. A ___ is a special arrangement or exhibit of products in a store.

8. Special displays of products are often placed at the end of an ___.

DOWN

1. ___ foods, such as bread and milk, are present in most kitchens.

3. A can of corn labeled only Corn is a ___ product.

4. ___ are trademark names of products put out by a certain company.

6. ___ are eaten at regular times, such as breakfast, lunch, etc.

EXAMPLES

Circle a letter to show *examples* of each category.

1. **Basic food items**

   a. salt, bread, margarine   b. peanuts, soda, cupcakes

2. **Meals**

   a. weekdays, weekends,   b. breakfast, lunch,
      late night   dinner

3. **Food products**

   a. paper towels, sponges,   b. muffins, orange juice,
      detergent   pickles

4. **Generic product brands**

   a. stewed tomatoes, peaches,   b. SuperStores, Good Deal,
      chili con carne   Cheapo

5. **Nationally advertised brands**

   a. Home Packed, Tasty,   b. Pillsbury, Birdseye,
      Fresh 'n' Fine   Kellogg

6. **Snack foods**

   a. pretzels, cookies,   b. cucumbers, pineapple,
      pork rinds   spaghetti

DRAWING CONCLUSIONS

Answer the questions in complete sentences.

1. Why isn't it a good idea to go grocery shopping when you're hungry?

   _____

   _____

2. Why do nationally advertised brands cost so much more
   than store brands?

   _____

   _____

3. Why is it a good idea to buy fresh fruits and vegetables when they're "in season"?

_____

_____

4. What should you watch out for when you're comparing the prices of two products?

_____

_____

SYNONYMS

First, unscramble the words. Then write each unscrambled word next to its *synonym* (word that means the same).

NAGECH _____	**UPSEARCH** _____
KERTAM _____	**STOYCL** _____
ERRIQUE _____	**OWL-STOC** _____

1. **Inexpensive**_____ generic foods can save you money.

2. List the ingredients you need to **buy** _____.

3. You might decide to **alter** _____ your menu.

4. Make a list before you go to the **store** _____.

5. Wise shoppers don't buy things they don't **need** _____.

6. Snack foods are usually the most **expensive** _____.

VEGETARIANISM

Before reading . . .

Why do some people choose *not* to eat meat? Is it possible to have a healthy diet without animal protein? This lesson will serve as a basic introduction to *vegetarianism*.

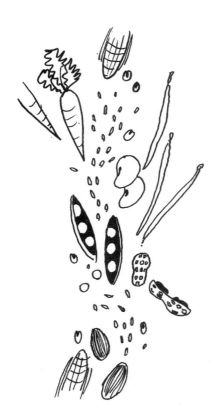

Many Americans are vegetarians. Vegetarians eat no fish, flesh, or fowl. Some refuse to eat any animal products, including eggs and milk. For most people, meat, eggs, and milk are chief sources of the protein needed by the body.

How do vegetarians get enough protein? Fortunately, many other foods, including vegetables, contain protein. A vegetarian's major sources of protein are beans, soy, nuts, rice, and other grains. Also, some foods eaten together have more protein than when eaten alone. For example, a mixture of beans and rice provides more protein than either food on its own.

There are different kinds of vegetarians. Those who eat no eggs or milk are called *vegans*. *Ovolactovegetarians* eat eggs (ovo) and milk (lacto) as well as vegetables, fruits, legumes, and grains. A *lactovegetarian* eats milk products but not eggs.

IS VEGETARIANISM A GOOD IDEA?

Arguments *For* Vegetarianism

- Some vegetarians believe that it is morally wrong to kill any animal for food.

- Other vegetarians believe that meat-eating is unnecessarily wasteful. They argue that the valuable land used for raising animals could feed many more people if it were used to grow crops of vegetables and grains.

The term *vegetarianism* was first used in 1847. The idea of such a diet, however, is hundreds of years old. Some people, particularly Hindus and Buddhists, eat only plant foods because of their religious beliefs.

- Still other vegetarians point out that meat animals are subject to dangerous diseases that could be harmful to humans. Many believe that human teeth are not well-adapted to chewing meat. They feel that this proves that humans were not intended to be flesh-eaters.

  According to their theories, all the nutrition necessary for a person's bodily and mental health can be provided by cereals, fruits, and vegetables.

Arguments *Against* Vegetarianism

- Opponents of vegetarianism argue that the human digestive system shows that humans were intended to live on a mixed diet. They point out that humans have grinding teeth for chewing vegetables as well as sharp teeth designed for tearing meat. Therefore, they reason, nature intended that the human diet should include both meat and vegetables. According to them, populations that exist on a "plants only" diet have not accomplished as much as those who are meat-eaters.

- Many scientists favor a mixed diet. Why? Animal proteins are complete proteins. They contain all the essential amino acids necessary for building muscle and other body tissues. Certain legumes, such as soybeans, do have relatively high protein value. But unless dietary protein is truly ample, human physical growth can be retarded.

COMPREHENSION

Answer the questions in complete sentences.

1. What are three different kinds of vegetarians?

_____

2. What are some sources of protein besides milk, eggs, and meat?

_____

3. What does the prefix lacto- mean?

_____

4. What two foods provide more protein in combination than separately?

_____

5. Why do some vegetarians make the claim that eating animals can be harmful to humans?

_____

6. What do animal proteins provide humans a complete supply of?

_____

SYNONYMS

Notice the **boldface** word in each phrase from the reading. Then add vowels (a, e, i, o, u) to complete a synonym (word that means the same or nearly the same) for each boldface word.

1. live on a **mixed** diet

   C___M B___N___D

2. for **tearing** meat

   R___P P___N G

3. were **intended** to live

   M___ ___N T

4. have not **accomplished**

   ___C H___ ___V___D

5. **favor** a mixed diet

   PR___F___R

6. high protein **value**

   C___N T___N T

7. **therefore**, nature intended

   T H___ S

8. **exist** on a diet

   L___V___

SUFFIX -ism

A *vegetarian* practices *vegetarianism*. The suffix *-ism* creates a new noun form. It shows action, a process, or a doctrine. Add the suffix *-ism* to the following words. Rewrite the words on the lines. Then write a letter to match each new word with its definition.

1. _____ **hero**
   _____

2. _____ **race**
   _____

3. _____ **sex**
   _____

4. _____ **capital**
   _____

5. _____ **hypnosis**
   _____

6. _____ **patriot**
   _____

7. _____ **alcohol**
   _____

a. economic system based on private ownership for profit

b. diseased condition; excessive desire to drink alcoholic liquor

c. act of putting people in a very relaxed, suggestible condition

d. quality and actions showing bravery and nobility

e. behavior based on the idea that one sex is superior

f. practice of discrimination and segregation on the basis of race

g. showing great love and loyalty for one's own country

SYLLABLES

Find one word in the reading that fits each description. First write the word on the line. Then break it up into syllables (separate sounds).

1. nine-syllable word: _____

   _____/_____/_____/_____/_____/_____/_____/_____/_____

2. six-syllable word: _____

   _____/_____/_____/_____/_____/_____

53

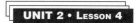

PUZZLER

Use the clues to help you complete the crossword puzzle.
Answers are words that complete the sentences.

ACROSS

1. ___ are seeds produced by cereal plants such as wheat.

4. ___ of vegetarianism think humans are well-adapted to meat eating.

6. ___ are plants with seeds that grow in pods.

7. ___ have relatively high protein value.

DOWN

1. ___ teeth in humans are adapted for chewing.

2. Complete proteins contain all essential ___ acids.

3. Should land be used for raising animals or for growing ___?

5. A ___ eats vegetables, fruits, grains, and legumes, but no meat, eggs, or milk.

CATEGORIES

Cross out the item that does *not* fit in each category.

1. Food items a vegan may eat:

   pineapple chunks   veal cutlets   carrot sticks

2. Religions that promote vegetarianism:

   Buddhism   Catholicism   Hinduism

3. Food items an ovolactovegetarian may eat:

   vegetable soup   bean burrito   tuna sandwich

4. Grains:

    barley   rye   pecans

5. Milk products:

    cottage cheese   butter   gravy

6. Food items a lactovegetarian may eat:

    omelette   tofuburgers   applesauce

SPELLING

Notice that the following words from the reading have been misspelled.
Write each word correctly on the line.

1. opponant _____

2. dietery _____

3. degestive _____

4. phisical _____

ANTONYMS

First unscramble the words from the reading. Then write each unscrambled
word below its *antonym* (word that means the opposite).

PALME _____	**TEENSAILS** _____
CEFHI _____	**DREADTER** _____
FLUMRAH _____	**NOWRG** _____

1. morally **right** to kill

   _____

2. growth is **accelerated**

   _____

3. **beneficial** to humans

   _____

4. **unnecessary** amino acids

   _____

5. truly **inadequate** protein

   _____

6. **minor** sources of protein

   _____

Unit 2 ————— REVIEW —————————

VOCABULARY

Unscramble the words to complete the sentences.

1. When your diet includes all four food groups, you get all the
    STINERNUT _____ you need.

2. Certain vitamins and minerals are **LENTSAISE** _____
    to your health.

3. **CEEGRIN** _____ foods are less expensive than foods
    with brand names.

4. Vegetarians must be careful to get enough **NEOTRIP**
    _____ in their diets.

MULTIPLE CHOICE

Circle a letter to complete each sentence.

1. Foods in the bread and cereal group give you vitamins,
    minerals, and
    a. macaroni.   b. protein.   c. calcium.   d. carbohydrates.

2. Vitamin D is often added to milk to help build stronger
    a. muscles and tendons.   c. hair and fingernails.
    b. teeth and bones.   d. skin and teeth.

3. To compare the prices of two products, you must first determine
    a. the length and width.   c. the size and shape.
    b. the price plus tax.   d. the price per ounce.

4. Two religions that promote vegetarianism are
    a. Mysticism and Hypnotism.   c. Veganism and Lactoveganism.
    b. Hinduism and Buddhism.   d. Capitalism and Socialism.

56

WORKING FOR A LIVING

LESSON 1: Today's Workplace
LESSON 2: Blue Collar/White Collar
LESSON 3: Preparing for a Job Interview
LESSON 4: Interviewing for a Job

When you complete the lessons in this unit, you will be able to answer questions like these:

■ *What kind of clothes should you **not** wear to a job interview?*

■ *What type of thinking skills are necessary in today's workplace?*

■ *What sort of training does a beginning carpenter need?*

■ *What kind of math skills does an auto salesperson need?*

PRETEST

Write **T** or **F** to show whether you think each statement is *true* or *false*.

1. _____ Today's workers can't be effective unless they can apply and expand on their basic knowledge.

2. _____ Most auto salespersons are paid on a commission basis.

3. _____ Never ask an interviewer how much the job pays until after the interview.

4. _____ Telling an interviewer about your family problems might help you get the job.

5. _____ You must be at least 17 years old to apply for a union apprenticeship.

6. _____ Many workers need strong writing skills in order to interact with machines.

Pretest answers: 1. T 2. T 3. F 4. F 5. T 6. T

TODAY'S WORKPLACE

Before reading . . .

In years gone by, workers were valued for their strong backs and willing hands. Weakness in basic academic skills was often ignored or kept hidden. Today's computerized workplace is much more demanding. This lesson discusses the higher skill levels that are now required of beginning workers.

America is a fortunate country. The vast majority of workers here are literate and numerate. But is basic knowledge enough? Today's workers can't be effective unless they can apply and expand on what they know.

Reading on the job only *begins* with the ability to decode words and understand the main idea. Today, workplace reading tasks are more demanding. Employers expect workers to analyze and summarize written material. They also require their employees to monitor their own comprehension and to use high-level thinking strategies to solve problems.

Today's employees are also expected to write well. In many jobs, writing is the first step in communicating with customers. In other jobs, skillful writing is required for interacting with machines or moving new ideas into the workplace. Workers in a wide range of jobs must be able to write detailed directions and explanations. To be successful, they need to "get their ideas down on paper" clearly and quickly.

Workplace math involves more than adding, subtracting, multiplying, and dividing. On the job, workers must use their basic math knowledge to identify and solve problems. They must be skilled at mathematical reasoning and estimation.

Today's employers depend on a workforce that has sound basic academic skills. Why? Without workers who are competent thinkers and communicators, businesses can't compete in the modern marketplace.

The U.S. Department of Labor has come up with an interesting statistic: On average, workers spend one and one-half to two hours per workday reading forms, charts, graphs, manuals, and so on. For many employees, writing is also part of the regular workday. And computation is used daily to conduct inventories, report on production levels, measure machine parts, and so on.

Employers can no longer afford to hire poorly educated workers. Employees with weak basic skills waste companies' money. They lower productivity, increase accident rates, and cause costly production errors.

COMPREHENSION

Write **T** or **F** to show whether the statement is *true* or *false*. Write **NI** if there is *no information* in the reading to help you make a judgment.

1. _____ Problem-solving is an important skill in most modern jobs.

2. _____ Writing is often the first step in communicating with customers.

3. _____ Workers who can't speak and write English well will soon be out of work.

4. _____ A knowledge of geography is becoming increasingly important in today's workplace.

SYLLABLES

Break the following words into syllables (separate sounds).

1. interact

   _____/_____/_____

2. ability

   _____/_____/_____/_____

3. communicate

   _____/_____/_____/_____

4. computerized

   _____/_____/_____/_____

5. estimate

   _____/_____/_____

6. analyze

   _____/_____/_____

SUFFIX *-ing*

Rewrite the words below, adding the suffix *-ing*. Hint: Before adding the suffix, you will have to add or delete one letter.

1. begin _____

2. compete _____

3. measure _____

4. write _____

VOCABULARY

Circle a letter to show the meaning of the **boldface** word or words.

1. Workplace math now requires **reasoning** and estimation skills.

   a. having a
      reason for
      your actions

   b. coming up
      with good
      excuses

   c. coming to a
      conclusion by
      considering facts

2. Today's employees must be **competent** communicators.

   a. having the
      ability to do
      what is needed

   b. comprehend
      every step of
      every job

   c. communicate
      with great
      feeling

3. Modern workers must have **sound** basic skills.

   a. noisy   b. audio   c. strong

60

4. Employers must try to prevent **costly production errors**

   a. unpopular   b. expensive   c. high-priced
      products   mistakes   parts

5. Workers with weak skills have **lower productivity**

   a. accomplish   b. have low   c. get lower
      less work   standards   salaries

6. Workers must be able to **analyze** written material.

   a. proofread   b. examine part   c. translate
      and edit   by part   into English

7. The ability to **decode** words is the most basic reading skill.

   a. sound out   b. make a code for   c. rhyme

DRAWING CONCLUSIONS

Use your own experience and ideas to answer the following questions.

1. Why might workers with weak basic skills increase
   accident rates?

   _____

   _____

   _____

2. What kind of materials might a worker need to read during
   a typical workday?

   _____

   _____

3. What kind of writing might a worker need to do during a
   typical workday?

   _____

   _____

PUZZLER

Use the clues to help you solve the crossword puzzle. Answers are words that complete the sentences.

ACROSS

2. Estimation is an important ___ skill.

4. You must ___ a problem before you can solve it.

6. Today's workers must be able to ___ what they know.

8. Employees must ___ their own comprehension of what they are reading.

9. You must not only know how to ___ words, but also understand what they mean.

DOWN

1. Weakness in academic ___ was once ignored.

3. Workers must have the ___ to write clearly.

5. Successful employees know how to ___ on their base of knowledge.

7. Companies can no longer afford workers who can't ___ problems.

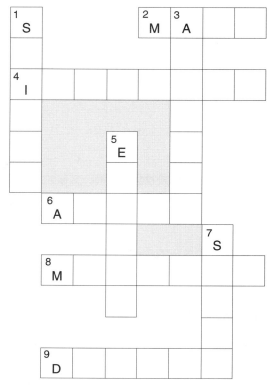

WORD COMPLETION

Use vowels (*a, e, i, o, u*) to complete the words from the reading.

1. America is a F__RT__N__T__ country.

2. Workplace R__ __D__NG tasks require thinking skill.

3. Writing is often the first step in C__MM__N__C__T__NG with customers.

4. Workers must write well in order to __NT__R__CT with machines.

5. Many workers read GR__PHS and M__N__ __LS on a daily basis.

WORD FORMS

Underline the word or words in each sentence that appears in the wrong *form*. Then rewrite the sentence, using the correct form of the word.

1. Businesses can't competition in the modern marketplace with poorly educated workers.

   _____

   _____

2. Were you surprised by the interesting statistical from the Department of Labor?

   _____

   _____

3. Today's workers must be able to summary written material.

   _____

   _____

4. High-level thinking strategy are required in the modern workplace.

   _____

   _____

5. Today, most American workers are literacy and numeral.

   _____

   _____

6. Compute skills are required to measure parts and conduct inventories.

   _____

   _____

BLUE COLLAR/WHITE COLLAR

Before reading . . .

Have you ever heard jobs described as "white collar" or "blue collar"? These terms are used to distinguish two broad categories of work. White-collar workers are clerks or professionals who usually work indoors. Blue-collar workers usually work with their hands in an industrial setting. This lesson introduces you to one job in each category.

BLUE-COLLAR JOB: CARPENTER

Carpenters build and repair things that are made out of wood. Some carpenters work on new buildings. They put up a building's framework as well as its walls and roof. They also install doors, windows, and floors. Some carpenters install cabinets, paneling, and molding.

Carpenters are hired to remodel rooms or buildings. Carpenters may also make things such as scaffolds and forms for concrete. They might even build large wooden bridges or piers. Some skilled carpenters do only fine woodwork. They specialize in making things like furniture, counters, and cabinets.

Carpenters must use many different skills on the job. They use math to measure things and to cut, shape, and join materials. They use reading skills to interpret plans, blueprints, and building codes. Carpenters must know how to use many kinds of hand and power tools. They must also know how to work safely and how to administer first aid.

Most employers recommend an apprenticeship as the best way to learn carpentry. These programs combine on-the-job training with related classroom instruction. Applicants for apprenticeships must be at least 17 years old and meet local union requirements. Some locals test an applicant's aptitude for carpentry. The length of the apprenticeship program, usually three to four years, may vary with the apprentice's skills.

Some beginning carpenters do not do apprenticeships. Instead, they get informal, on-the-job training directly from employers. The quality and degree of training may not be as high, however.

Young people interested in carpentry should take high school courses in woodshop, mechanical drawing, and general mathematics. They should have good manual dexterity and eye-hand coordination. The ability to solve arithmetic problems quickly and accurately is very important.

WHITE-COLLAR JOB: AUTO SALESPERSON

Auto salespeople may sell new cars in a showroom or previously owned cars on a used car lot. They greet potential customers, show them cars that may meet their needs, and help them decide on a purchase. If they sell new cars, auto sales workers may place orders for the models their customers want and draw up the necessary papers. They must understand finance contracts and know something about auto insurance.

Like successful salespeople in any field, auto sales workers must know their business. To gain their customers' respect, they must be able to answer questions knowledgeably. Cars are very high-priced goods. Customers like to feel they can trust their salesperson's judgment.

A good appearance and a pleasant manner are important to the success of an auto sales worker. The ability to speak well in person and over the telephone can make the difference between gaining and losing a sale.

Auto sales workers usually get on-the-job training. They learn to make sales presentations and to "close" sales by observing experienced workers and by practicing. Most auto salespersons are paid on a commission basis. This means that they earn a percentage of the price of the cars they sell. On used cars, they may earn a share of the dealer's profit on the sale. Many dealers pay their commissioned sales workers a small weekly or monthly salary so that they will have a steady income.

Sometimes auto salespersons go for weeks without making a sale. This can be very discouraging. Sales workers must be able to maintain their self-confidence and determination during such slack periods.

COMPREHENSION

Answer the questions in complete sentences.

1. What three high school classes would be especially useful to someone interested in carpentry?

   _____

   _____

2. Why does a car buyer need to be able to trust a salesperson's judgment?

   _____

   _____

3. Cars that have been previously owned are usually called by what name?

   _____

4. What is a carpenter's period of formal training called?

   _____

5. Which job described in the reading would be most difficult for a very shy person?

   _____

6. What term is used in both job descriptions to describe training that is not formal?

   _____

DRAWING CONCLUSIONS

Cross out the personal characteristic that would *not* be particularly important in each job.

1. **carpenter**   strong   flexible   accurate   talkative

2. **salesperson**   determined   charming   artistic   well-groomed

PUZZLER

Use the clues to help you solve the crossword puzzle. Answers are words that complete the sentences.

ACROSS

1. Applicants for apprenticeships may have to take an ___ test.

3. Carpenters must solve arithmetic problems quickly and ___.

6. The ___ may pay an auto salesperson a small weekly salary.

8. Sales workers must keep up their confidence during ___ periods.

DOWN

2. Salespeople are paid a ___ of the price of the cars they sell.

4. An ___ carpenter usually trains for three to four years.

5. Auto sales workers who "know their business" earn the customer's ___.

7. Carpenters use many different hand and power ___.

VOCABULARY

Circle a letter to show the meaning of the **boldface** word or words.

1. An auto salesperson must greet **potential** customers.

   a. talented   b. possible   c. nervous

2. Cars are very high-priced **goods**.

   a. items for sale   b. perfect products   c. luxury vehicles

3. Some carpenters build bridges and **piers**.

   a. high, pointed towers   b. sidewalks made of wooden slats   c. structures on pillars built over water

4. People who want to be carpenters should have good **manual dexterity**

    a. ability to   b. skillful use   c. manufacturing
         read manuals   of the hands   skills

5. An auto sales worker must be able to make a good **presentation**

    a. introduction of   b. give customers   c. the lowest
         the car's best   a small gift   possible sales
         features   price

6. Sales workers must **maintain** their self-confidence.

    a. develop   b. preserve   c. pretend

7. Some carpenters install paneling and **molding.**

    a. fuzzy growth   b. shaped wooden   c. strips that make
         caused by a   strip around a   up a hardwood
         fungus   wall or door   floor

8. Most auto salespersons are paid on a **commission basis**

    a. by a committee   b. are committed   c. receive money when
         of customers   to their employers   a sale is made

COMPOUND WORDS

Write a compound word to complete each sentence. Choose the first part of the compound from List A and the second part from List B. Hint: You will *not* use all the words, and you will use some words twice.

LIST A	
blue	sales
some	class
frame	show
self	wood

LIST B	
person	prints
thing	work
room	where
confidence	people

1. Those who sell new cars must know _____ about auto insurance.

2. Apprentice carpenters learn how to read _____.

3. Sales workers need to maintain their _____ during slack periods.

4. It takes skilled carpentry to do fine _____.

5. New cars are usually displayed in a _____.

6. Auto _____ earn a share of the dealer's profit on a used car sale.

7. Carpenters put up the _____ of a new building.

8. A successful auto _____ has a pleasant manner and a good appearance.

SYLLABLES

Break the **boldface** words into syllables (separate sounds).

determination	knowledgeably	observing	commission
recommend	apprenticeship	presentation	previously

_____/_____/_____   _____/_____/_____/_____

_____/_____/_____/_____   _____/_____/_____

_____/_____/_____   _____/_____/_____/_____/_____

_____/_____/_____/_____   _____/_____/_____/_____

MULTIPLE-MEANING WORDS

Many words have different meanings in different contexts. Circle a letter to show the meaning of the **boldface** word as it is used in the sentence.

1. Carpenters know how to cut, shape, and **join** building materials.

   a. sign up as a member
   b. connect or fasten together
   c. accompany someone else

2. A small salary gives sales workers a **steady** income.

   a. regular, ongoing
   b. balanced; not shaky
   c. serious, sensible

3. Applicants for apprenticeships must **meet** local requirements.

   a. be formally introduced to
   b. keep a scheduled appointment with
   c. satisfy, fulfill

LESSON 3

PREPARING FOR A JOB INTERVIEW

Before reading . . .

How can you make a good impression on a job interview? *Getting ready* for the interview can be just as important as the interview itself. Thorough preparation means thinking ahead and trying to see yourself through an employer's eyes.

1. **Be sure to bring with you:**

   - A card or piece of paper listing all the information you'll need to fill out a job application (date of birth, Social Security number, names, addresses, and phone numbers of references, etc.)

   - Your own pen. You may need it to fill in forms.

   - Any special documents you may need such as licenses, diplomas, certificates, and work permits.

   - A list of questions you would like to have answered. The questions might be about salary, benefits, working conditions, etc.

   - The name and title of the person whom you are supposed to see (if you made an appointment in advance).

2. **Prepare for any tests you may have to take.**

   - Practice typing if you are going for a keyboarding job.

   - Brush up on your arithmetic if you are going for a job that requires handling money or using figures and measurements.

   - Get in shape or take whatever training you may need if you have to pass a test of physical strength or agility.

   - Practice taking tests so the real thing won't shake you. Remember—half the battle in any test is staying confident!

3. **Make sure you can get to the interview on time, and that you have a way to get there.**

   - Get a schedule if you are going to be using public transportation.

   - If you are driving, make sure you know the way. Check a map ahead of time. If someone else will be doing the driving, make sure that person will be able to wait for you!

   - If your interview is set for a certain time, make a dry run to see how long the trip will take.

4. **Find out all you can about the job and the employer.** This will show the interviewer that you are sincerely interested in the job. It will also help you to ask good questions and to better understand the answers you get.

You might want to know:

- what the employer makes or does,
- how long the company has been in business,
- how many employees work there,
- how well the business is doing, and
- what the chances are for moving up on the job.

5. **Figure out how much money you need to earn before you go for the interview.** Then you will know if the salary being offered will be enough for you.

6. **Look your best.**

- Take a bath or shower.
- Wash your hair.
- Brush your teeth.
- Men should shave. (Don't use strong after-shave lotions.)
- Women should be careful not to use too much perfume or makeup.
- Get a good night's sleep so you will look fresh and rested.

7. **Dress properly for the interview.**

- Dress simply. Avoid wild styles and too much flashy jewelry.
- For office jobs and most public-contact jobs, dress the way most office workers do. Men wear clean shirts and slacks and perhaps a jacket and tie. Women wear dresses or skirts and blouses.

- If there is a chance that you might be asked to start work right away, wear work clothes to the interview.
- Whatever you wear, make sure your clothes are clean and neat and suitable for the place where the interview is to take place.

8. **Think about your priorities.**

- How important is it to have your nights and weekends free?
- Do you live too far from the workplace to make a reasonable commute?
- Would you enjoy working downtown? In a factory district? Only in a quiet place?

9. **Make sure you have a positive attitude.** Keep all your good points in mind. Be prepared to talk about them. Remember, if you don't appear to be confident in yourself, you can't expect others to have confidence in you. But don't get carried away! It is bad manners to brag or show off.

10. **Confirm your appointment.** Take one more step if you must travel a long way to get there. Call the day before to doublecheck that the person you are supposed to see will be there to see you.

COMPREHENSION

Write **T** or **F** to show whether each statement is *true* or *false*.

1. _____ When you get hired, your new employer will issue you a Social Security number.

2. _____ Being late for a job interview shows that you may be an unreliable employee.

3. _____ An employer might contact your references to ask about your work habits.

4. _____ The interviewer will think you are nosy if you ask too many questions about the job.

SYNONYMS

Find a *synonym* (word that means the same) in the box for each **boldface** word. Write the synonym on the line. Hint: You will *not* use all the words in the box.

exam	appropriately	boss	affordably	commute
ride	department	rumors	business	inquiries

1. Be sure to dress **properly** for a job interview. _____

2. Your good **questions** show the interviewer that you are sincerely interested in the job. _____

3. An employer may give you a **test** to see if your job skills are strong. _____

4. You might ask the interviewer how many employees work for the **company**. _____

5. Figure out how far you'd have to **travel** to get from your home to the workplace. _____

PUZZLER

Use the clues to help you complete the crossword puzzle.

ACROSS

4. official written records

5. arrangement to meet someone at a certain time and place

6. ability to move with quickness and ease

7. a set of questions or problems for finding out how knowledgeable or skilled a person is

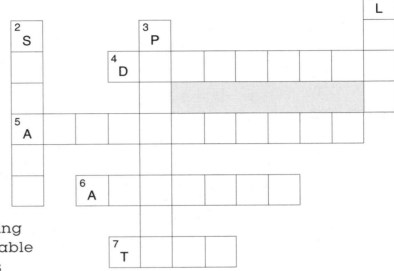

DOWN

1. a series of words, numbers, etc. set down in order

2. the fixed amount of money regularly paid to a worker

3. attitude that is assured, hopeful, confident

FIGURATIVE LANGUAGE

Circle a letter to show the meaning of the **boldfaced** words.

1. **Brush up on** your arithmetic if you are going for a job that requires handling money.

   a. comb your hair flat
   b. review and practice
   c. ask for help with

2. The day before the interview, **make a dry run** to see how long the trip will take.

   a. jog from your home to the workplace
   b. use a dry marker on a map
   c. time how long it takes to get there

3. Ask about your chances for **moving up** in the company.

   a. being promoted to a better job
   b. being number one in line
   c. taking the boss's job

4. Be prepared to talk about your **good points**

   a. your skill at hunting and fishing
   b. your generosity and kindness
   c. your strengths as an employee

5. Don't **get carried away** when you say positive things about yourself.

    a. let your thoughts wander   b. sound as if you're boasting   c. escorted by security guards

6. Practice taking tests so the real thing won't **shake** you.

    a. make you nervous   b. push you around   c. build your confidence

SUFFIXES

Underline the word in each sentence that needs a *suffix*. Then rewrite the word on the line, adding a suffix from the box. Hint: You will *not* use all the suffixes, and some will be used more than once.

-ing	-ity	-ation	-ences	-able	-ment
-ly	-ist	-ants	-ible	-sion	-ry

1. List your inform on a piece of paper.   _____

2. Show that you are sincere interested in the job.   _____

3. Bring the names and addresses of your refer.   _____

4. If you are drive, make sure you know the way.   _____

5. Does the job require handle money?   _____

6. Be on time for your appoint.   _____

7. Dress simple for the interview.   _____

8. Don't wear a lot of jewel.   _____

9. Are your clothes suit for the workplace?   _____

10. Some jobs require physical agile.   _____

VOCABULARY

Circle a letter to show the meaning of the **boldface** word.

1. Get a **schedule** if you will be using public transportation.

    a. flowchart showing steps in a process   b. timetable of departures and arrivals

2. Did you make your interview appointment **in advance**?
   a. ahead of time   b. too early in the day

3. To you, what are the **priorities** in a job?
   a. earlier commitments   b. most important factors

EXAMPLES

Circle two examples of each **boldface** word or phrase.

1. **public-contact jobs**
   warehouse worker   salesperson   custodian   waitress   plumber

2. **arithmetic**
   subtraction   explanation   permission   division   grammar

3. **benefits**
   promotion   sick leave   vacation   salary   schedule

4. **documents**
   confidence   appointment   license   diploma   map

5. **office workers**
   mechanic   receptionist   chef   landscaper   accountant

6. **job titles**
   manager   sir   Mrs.   president   lady   employee

7. **public transportation**
   helicopter   bus   sidewalks   subway   pickup truck

INFERENCE

Answer the questions in complete sentences.

1. Why should you take your own pen to an interview?

   _____

2. Why should you check a map before driving to an interview?

   _____

3. Why should women be careful not to wear too much perfume?

   _____

75

INTERVIEWING FOR A JOB

Before reading . . .

Applying for a job can be stressful. But staying cool and calm is the secret of a successful job interview. The *dos* and *don'ts* in this lesson can help you overcome nervousness and conduct yourself in a confident, businesslike manner.

1. **Be on time for the interview.** Arrive 5 or 10 minutes early to get yourself together.

2. **Don't get there *too* early.** Waiting too long might make you more nervous. If you are early, ask for directions to the restroom. Go there and freshen up your appearance.

3. **If you come with a friend, the friend should wait outside the building.** Only children need someone with them all the time. An employer will not give a job to a child. Show that you can do things on your own.

4. **Be on your best behavior from the moment you walk in the door.** The receptionist to whom you speak may take part in the interview process. After you leave, she may be asked what she thinks of you. Some of the other employees may be looking you over, too. Be friendly—but not *too* friendly.

5. **Take a close look around you.** Try to get some idea of the way the employer treats the employees. Ask yourself if this is the kind of place you would like to work.

6. **If you have been eating before the interview, chew a breath freshener.**

7. **Make sure you understand what you are supposed to do if you are taking a test or filling out an application form.** Politely ask the person in charge to explain anything you don't understand. Don't try to get help from other job applicants. And don't get frustrated or nervous. Just stay calm and do your best.

8. **Smile and be friendly when you meet the interviewer.** Walk tall and stand straight, with your head up. Greet the interviewer in a confident, respectful way. Reach out to shake hands and give the interviewer your name.

   When you shake hands, be firm. But be careful. Don't try to show how strong you are.

9. **Speak out in a clear, strong voice.** Do not use street talk. Take your time. Try to watch your grammar, and don't mumble your words. How you speak is usually more important for office work than for other kinds of work. But speaking well always makes a good impression on an interviewer.

10. **Look straight at the interviewer as much as possible.** Don't fidget or move around the room. Wait until the interviewer asks you to sit down before you take a seat. When you do sit down, sit up straight with both feet on the floor. Keep your legs together. In other words—make yourself comfortable, but don't slouch.

11. **Don't chew gum or ask the interviewer for permission to smoke.**

12. **Listen carefully to everything the interviewer has to say.** Don't interrupt. Answer questions as fully as you can.

13. **If you have some things on your application form that should be explained, do it right away.** This is important in such matters as an arrest record or bad health. In fact, it is better to write "to be explained" on your application than to fill in such information.

14. **Don't try to control the interview.** Except for explaining important problems not treated on your application form, let the interviewer direct the interview. Wait until he or she asks if you have any questions. Then you can bring up anything that has not been covered.

15. **Don't bring up personal, family, or money problems.** They are not going to make the interviewer feel sorry for you and give you a job. In fact, telling about your problems usually turns the interviewer off.

16. **Show yourself to be reasonable.** Say that you are willing to start low and work yourself up as you learn more about the work. Don't tell the interviewer that you must have this or that privilege or else you won't take the job.

17. **Don't try to get *too* friendly with the interviewer.** Never call interviewers by their first names, even if they use your first name.

18. **Don't forget that the last impression you give may be as important as the first impression.** Try to close the interview well. Usually, the interviewer will signal when it is time for you to go. He or she may stand up and thank you for coming in.

It takes time for someone to follow up on the information you gave on your application form. So don't expect to learn if you have the job for several days or even weeks.

19. **Thank the interviewer for seeing you.** Shake hands the same way you did at the beginning of the interview. Then leave—walking out as straight as you entered.

20. **If you are interested in the job, write or call the interviewer within the next day or so.** Keep the call or letter short and simple. Just thank the interviewer again for visiting with you. Say once again that you are interested in the job.

COMPREHENSION

Circle the word or words that correctly complete each sentence.

1. The clothes you wear to a job interview must be
   (fashionable and expensive / clean and neat).

2. You will make a better impression if you are a bit
   (tardy / early) for your interview.

3. Never (wear glasses / chew gum) while you are being
   interviewed for a job.

4. Interviewers prefer job applicants who seem
   (friendly and cheerful / talkative and aggressive).

5. If something on your application needs to be explained, do it
   (after you're hired / right away).

6. It is the job of the (applicant / interviewer) to control the
   interview.

7. When the interviewer stands up, it usually means that
   (you won't get the job / the interview is over).

8. An interviewer will not give you a job because he or she
   (feels sorry for you / thinks you listen carefully).

SPELLING

First, underline the misspelled word in each sentence. Then spell the word
correctly on the line.

1. Watch your grammer. _____

2. Don't interupt the interviewer. _____

3. Don't bring a freind with you. _____

4. Allways shake hands firmly. _____

CAUSE AND EFFECT

Circle either *cause* or *effect* to correctly complete each sentence.

1. Increased nervousness might be (a **cause** / an **effect**) of arriving too early for a job interview.

2. Complaining to an interviewer about your personal problems could be (a **cause** / an **effect**) of not being hired.

3. Writing a polite follow-up note after an interview might be (a **cause** / an **effect**) of being hired.

4. Mumbling your words might be (a **cause** / an **effect**) of making a bad impression.

INFERENCE

After a job interview, you may not find out if you have the job for several days or even weeks. Give two possible reasons for this delay.

1. _____

2. _____

FIGURATIVE LANGUAGE

Circle a letter to show the meaning of the **boldface** word or words.

1. The interviewer wants to know how you would **get along with** other employees.

   a. ride to work in a carpool
   b. cooperate and work agreeably with
   c. become best friends with

2. If you are **in the running for** the job, the interviewer may tell you so.

   a. moving fast enough
   b. an unlikely applicant for
   c. being seriously considered for

3. Interviewers are usually **turned off** when an applicant talks about money problems.

   a. stopped short
   b. sympathetic with
   c. unfavorably impressed

PUZZLER

Use the clues to help you complete the crossword puzzle.

ACROSS

2. the correct use of words in phrases and sentences

5. self-assured; certain

6. to move about in a nervous, restless way

7. work you are hired to do (plural)

DOWN

1. to sit or stand with the head dropping and the shoulders slumped

2. flavorful, sticky substance some people like to chew

3. form filled out by job-seekers

4. agitated; uneasy; tense

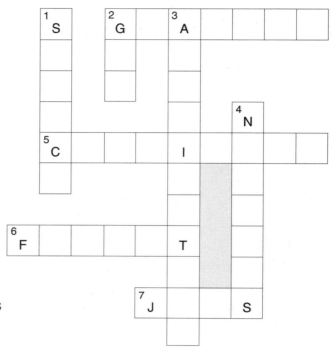

COMPOUND WORDS

Use words from the box to complete the *compound words* in the sentences.
Hint: You will *not* use all the words in the box.

stop	one	your	in	room	thing	some	out

1. You can go to the **rest**_____ to freshen up your appearance.

2. Have your friend wait _____**side** the building.

3. Arriving a few minutes early gives you a chance to get _____**self** together.

4. _____**one** at the company will follow up on the information you gave on your application.

SYNONYMS AND ANTONYMS

Look at the **boldface** word in each sentence. Then look in the box for a word that means the same or a word that means the opposite. Write the *synonym* or *antonym* on the line. Hint: You will *not* use all the words in the box.

encouraged	elaborate	hostile	personal
irrational	plain	completely	promptly
chummy	accurate	courteously	rudely

1. Be **friendly** with all the employees you meet in the workplace.   antonym: _____

2. **Politely** ask the person in charge to explain anything you don't understand.   synonym: _____

3. If you have to take a test, try not to get **frustrated** or nervous.   antonym: _____

4. Answer questions as **fully** as you can.   synonym: _____

5. Being **reasonable** during your interview indicates that you can get along with people.   antonym: _____

6. Be sure to keep your follow-up phone call short and **simple**.   antonym: _____

FORMS OF A WORD

To complete each sentence, write the correct *form* of each **boldfaced** word.

1. There are usually several **(apply)** _____ who interview for the same job.

2. All companies try to **(employment)**_____ workers who are skilled and dependable.

3. Sit up **(straightness)**_____, with both feet on the ground.

4. Listen **(careful)** _____ to what the interviewer has to say.

VOCABULARY

Unscramble the words to complete the sentences.

1. Today's workers must be able to find **TOULOSINS**

   _____ to problems in the workplace.

2. An **EPRICEPANT** _____ is still in the process

   of learning a trade.

3. Arrive a little early for your interview **MENPAINTPOT**

   _____.

4. Good eye contact shows confidence and makes a good

   NOISERIMPS _____ on the interviewer.

MULTIPLE CHOICE

Circle a letter to answer complete each sentence.

1. Employees with weak academic skills tend to

   a. lower productivity.   c. make costly errors.

   b. cause accidents.   d. all of the above

2. An important characteristic for an auto salesperson would be

   a. manual dexterity.   c. positive personality.

   b. physical strength.   d. eye-hand coordination.

3. To be ready to fill out a job application, you may need

   a. addresses and phone   c. permission from parents
      numbers of your references.   and teachers.

   b. pens with different   d. to study a bus schedule
      colors of ink.   and route map.

4. When you talk to an interviewer, you should

   a. watch your grammar.   c. speak in a clear, strong voice.

   b. avoid using street talk.   d. all of the above

PREVIEW

MANAGING YOUR MONEY

LESSON 1: Budgeting
LESSON 2: Applying for a Credit Card
LESSON 3: Cash or Credit?
LESSON 4: Borrowing Money

When you complete the lessons in this unit, you will be able to answer questions like these:

- *What responsibility comes with the freedom to make your own choices?*

- *How do creditors judge whether or not a customer will be **trustworthy**?*

- *How can self-knowledge keep you out of "money trouble"?*

- *Where are you likely to get the lowest interest rate on a loan?*

PRETEST

Write **T** or **F** to show whether you think each statement is *true* or *false*.

1. _____ Experts say that savings should be the number one item on your budget.

2. _____ Using a credit card is ideal for people who like to buy on impulse.

3. _____ No interest will be charged if you pay off your credit card bill within 60 days.

4. _____ The first step in making a budget is to get clear about the difference between your wants and needs.

5. _____ The total cost of a five-year loan is much more than the cost of a three-year loan.

6. _____ A low monthly payment is always more important than a low interest rate.

Pretest answers: 1. T 2. F 3. F 4. T 5. T 6. F

BUDGETING

Before reading . . .

Does money tend to "slip through your fingers"? Do you worry about not being able to pay for the things you really need? If so, the information in this lesson can help you control your money so it will be there when you really need it.

Many young people resist the word *budget*. They worry that "living on a budget" means pinching pennies and never having any fun. But a budget is actually nothing more than a simple plan for spending and saving money. It's an important way to take charge of your life so you *won't* have to worry about money!

A budget has three main parts. The first part is made up of *fixed expenses*. These are the things you *must* pay for every month. **Examples:** rent, food, transportation to school or work, etc.

The second part is the amount you have decided to *save* every month. Usually, people put away regular savings for very expensive things. **Examples:** a college education, a car, etc.

The third part of your budget is made up of *variable expenses*. These are costs that change in amount or do not come up every month. **Examples:** car repair, a summer vacation, a particularly high winter heating bill.

Give it a try. Add up the three parts of your monthly budget to find your total expenses. This amount can be called your *outgo*. Now compare your outgo to your regular monthly income.

Is your income very nearly the same as your outgo? If so, you have what is called a *balanced budget*.

A WORD TO THE WISE

Most young people are eager to get out on their own—to live independently. They want the freedom to make their own choices. Yet responsibility always comes with freedom. Financial independence will not be possible without the skills it takes to manage money wisely.

Is your income greater than your outgo? If so, you might put more money in savings or allow yourself extra money for recreation.

Is your planned outgo more than your income? The obvious solution is to find ways to cut your variable expenses.

All of us have to revise our budgets now and then. Sometimes we need to add another item or two. Sometimes our income changes. So don't be upset if the first draft of your budget doesn't work. Any reasonable spending plan can be adjusted as conditions change.

Remember that your goal is to *balance* expenses and income. Unless you can raise your income, you may have to trim the variable expenses in your outgo. Choosing which items to cut can be a challenge.

First, try to get very clear about the difference between your *wants* and your *needs*. Which budget items are which? Basic groceries, for example, are a need. Going to a movie every Friday night might be something you want to do, but can you really afford it? Movies are not things you really *need*, like food or water.

How could you reduce that expense? Perhaps you could take in a movie twice a month instead of every week. Or think about saving several dollars by going to a matinee instead of an evening show.

Making and keeping a budget does take some work. These tasks are well worth it in the long run, however. Here are a few tips to help you succeed:

- Keep good records of your income and expenses.

- Keep working on your spending plan until it fits the way you really live.

- Review your budget at the same time and in the same place every week.

- To motivate yourself, make lists of both your short-term and long-term financial goals.

COMPREHENSION

Write **T** or **F** to show whether a statement is *true* or *false*. Write **NI** if there is *no information* in the reading to help you make a judgment.

1. _____ A savings account only makes sense if you have extra money.

2. _____ In a balanced budget, your fixed expenses are no more than your variable expenses.

3. _____ As the circumstances of your life change, your budget may need to be adjusted.

4. _____ Financial counselors agree that all wage-earners should save at least 10 percent of their salaries.

5. _____ A budget has four main parts.

6. _____ Sharing your apartment with a roommate would reduce your fixed expenses.

7. _____ A miser is someone who never spends a penny.

SYNONYMS

Circle a letter to show the *synonym* (word that means the same) of the **boldface** word.

1. Sticking to a savings plan develops your **self-discipline**

   a. self-appointed   b. self-confidence   c. self-control

2. The first part of a budget lists **fixed** expenses.

   a. repaired   b. firm; regular   c. chemically treated

3. The second part of your budget is the **amount** you've decided to save.

   a. sum   b. leftover   c. percentage

4. **Variable** expenses make up the third part of your budget.

   a. unnecessary   b. a variety of   c. changeable

5. The first **draft** of your budget may not work very well.

   a. version   b. bank check   c. air current

6. Unless you can **raise** your income, you must trim variable expenses.

    a. make louder   b. increase   c. construct

7. You may well have to **revise** your budget now and then.

    a. proofread   b. review   c. rework

8. Which variable **expense** can you cut from your budget?

    a. cost   b. luxury   c. waste

9. Any **reasonable** spending plan must be somewhat flexible.

    a. motivated   b. sensible   c. explainable

10. **Chronic** financial problems are usually caused by poor planning.

    a. correctable   b. unforgivable   c. continual

SYLLABLES

Break the **boldfaced** words into syllables (separate sounds).

motivate	records	succeed	financial	item	conditions

1. _____/_____   2. _____/_____/_____

    _____/_____   _____/_____/_____

    _____/_____   _____/_____/_____

DRAWING CONCLUSIONS

Answer the questions in complete sentences.

1. What is a "nest egg"?

    _____

2. What do people mean when they say that money "slips through their fingers"?

    _____

PUZZLER

Use the clues to help you solve the crossword puzzle.

ACROSS

2. money you receive from all sources

5. not consistent; changing

7. to rewrite; make a second draft

8. ability achieved through training and willpower

DOWN

1. tending to be permanent; unlikely to change

3. to direct or have charge of

4. something you're hoping to achieve

6. a plan for spending and saving

ANTONYMS

Draw a line to match each **boldface** word with its *antonym* (word that means the opposite) on the right.

1. **short-term** goals

    a. occasional

2. to **pinch pennies**

    b. increase

3. **trim** expenses

    c. long-term

4. **regular** income

    d. spend lavishly

CATEGORIES

List each item in the box under the correct heading.

bus tokens	**donuts**	**water bill**	**birthday present**
car payment	**groceries**	**nail polish**	**roof repair**

1.   **FIXED EXPENSES**   2.   **VARIABLE EXPENSES**

_____   _____

_____   _____

_____   _____

_____   _____

WORD COMPLETION

Add vowels (*a, e, i, o, u*) to complete the incomplete words in each sentence.

1. R__SP__NS__B__L__T__ __S always go along with freedom.

2. Financial __ND__P__ND__NC__ is impossible without money management skills.

3. The three parts of your monthly budget added together make up your __ __TG__.

4. As a budget item, savings should be your top PR__ __R__TY.

5. A car R__P__ __R is an example of a variable expense.

6. If you have a B__L__NC__D budget, your income matches your outgo.

APPLYING FOR A CREDIT CARD

Before reading . . .

Are you *creditworthy*? If you applied for a credit card, could a lender trust you to pay for the goods and services you charge? This lesson will introduce you to some basic facts about qualifying for a credit card.

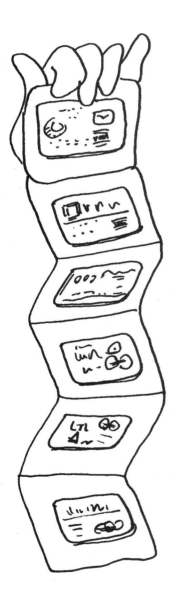

QUESTIONS CREDITORS ASK

Creditors are businesses that trust you to buy now and pay later. They earn money from the interest charges their customers pay. Creditors want to be sure that you will be able to pay your bills plus the interest. So they only extend credit to trustworthy people. Creditors will make this judgment by considering several factors.

WHAT ARE YOUR INCOME AND EXPENSES?

The first thing creditors will look at is your income. They will want to know the amount of your take-home pay. Next, they will look at your living expenses. This will include your rent, food, utilities, and so on. They will also want to know if you support other people. Then they will consider how much money is left after you have paid these basic expenses. This is the part of your income that determines whether or not you get credit.

WHAT OTHER SOURCES OF INCOME DO YOU HAVE?

Creditors will want to know if you own your own home. They will also want to find out if you have any other income from property, stocks, or savings.

HOW OLD ARE YOU?

Creditors will look at your age. You must be at least 18 years old to be legally responsible for your own debts. People under 18—and older people with no credit history or a history of poor credit use—will be required to have a responsible co-signer.

ARE YOU A GOOD CREDIT RISK?

Creditors will want to know if you are a good risk. They will want to know how long you have worked at your job. They will also want to know how long you have lived at your address. People who don't move around a lot are usually considered to be better credit risks.

HOW GOOD IS YOUR DEBT RECORD?

Next, creditors will look at your debt record. They will want to know if you have used credit before. They will also want to know if you paid off your balance, and if you paid it on time. Of course, creditors will ask if you have ever failed to pay your bills. This includes your rent or things like your telephone bill. Creditors will want to know how well you manage your money.

WHAT ARE YOUR PERSONAL HABITS?

Creditors will also judge you on a personal basis. They will think about the following things: Do you seem mature? Do you understand what credit is? Have you proved that you are willing to take on responsibility? Are you able and willing to pay back your loans and charges?

CREDIT REPORTING AGENCIES

Once you apply for credit, your name will be put on file. The creditor will report your name and all the information about you. A credit reporting agency will open a file on you. This credit file will last the rest of your life. Your file will be updated all the time.

All creditors use credit reporting agencies. It is an easy way for them to learn about your financial background.

If you are denied credit because of a report by a credit reporting agency, there are some steps you can take. By law, the creditor must tell you the name and address of the credit reporting agency that gave the report. Then you can write to ask for a copy. But you must do this within 30 days of being denied credit. The agency must give you a copy of the report free of charge.

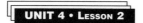

COMPREHENSION

Write **T** if the statement is *true* and **F** if the statement is *false*.
Write **NI** for *no information* if the article does not provide the facts
you need to make a judgment.

1. _____ By law, creditors must issue a credit card to any American
who needs one.

2. _____ Your living expenses include items such as rent and food.

3. _____ A wealthy teenager, such as a rock star, could probably
get a credit card without a co-signer.

4. _____ Many companies will not extend credit to teenagers.

5. _____ Creditors offer lower interest rates to students who get
good grades.

6. _____ Creditors prefer customers who have lived in the
community for a long time.

7. _____ The amount of your take-home pay determines whether
or not you will get credit.

VOCABULARY

Draw a line to match each term on the left with its meaning on the right.

1. **good risk**   a. valuable possessions

2. **stocks**   b. earnings after deductions

3. **property**   c. shares in a business

4. **take-home pay**   d. borrower who seems trustworthy

PUZZLER

Use the clues to help you solve the crossword puzzle.

ACROSS

1. to earn a living for someone

3. to take a chance on

6. a business that extends credit

7. amounts you spend

8. sensible, stable; not childish

DOWN

2. dependable and trustworthy

4. money you regularly receive

5. charges you pay for buying first and paying later

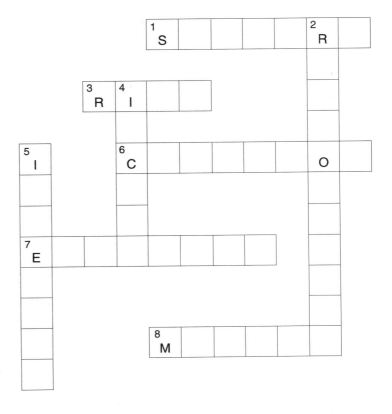

SYLLABLES

Break each word from the reading into syllables (separate sounds).

1. amount

   (_____/_____)

2. credit

   (_____/_____)

3. customer

   (_____/_____/_____)

4. property

   (_____/_____/_____)

5. original

   (_____/_____/_____/_____)

6. utilities

   (_____/_____/_____/_____)

SUFFIX *-ing*

Add *-ing* to the following verbs. Remember to drop the final *e* before adding a suffix to verbs that end in *e*.

1. **pay** _____

2. **include** _____

3. **show** _____

4. **have** _____

5. **lend** _____

6. **manage** _____

7. **consider** _____

8. **live** _____

9. **determine** _____

10. **borrow** _____

SPELLING

Underline *two* misspelled words in each sentence. Then rewrite the sentences correctly.

1. Credittors are bussineses that allow you to buy now and pay later.

   _____

2. Debters must pay for the goods they buy plus interst.

   _____

3. You must be 18 years old to be legaly responsable for your debts.

   _____

4. Creditors want to no how long you have lived at your adress.

   _____

SENTENCE COMPLETION

Unscramble the words to correctly complete the sentences.

1. Your name will be put on file when you **PYLPA** _____ for credit.

2. A credit reporting **YECNAG** _____ will open a file on you.

3. You must ask for a copy of the report within 30 days of being **NEEDID** _____ credit.

4. The agency must give you a free copy of your credit **TORPER** _____.

PARTS OF SPEECH

A word's part of speech depends on how it is used in a sentence. Many words can be used as either *nouns* or *verbs*. Remember that nouns name people, places, or things. Verbs tell about action or being.

First, write *noun* or *verb* to show how each **boldface** word is used in the sentence. If you write *verb*, write another sentence using the same word as a noun. If you write *noun*, use the word as a verb in the sentence you write.

1. Your credit **file** will last all your life.   _____

   _____

2. She needs $200 to pay the **rent**.   _____

   _____

3. He **charges** too much on his credit card.   _____

   _____

4. Do you think you are a good credit **risk**?   _____

   _____

CASH OR CREDIT?

Before reading . . .

Successful money management takes discipline and self-control. Are you mature enough to control your use of a credit card? This lesson will give you some tips about using credit wisely.

SHOULD I USE MY CREDIT CARD?

The smartest time to use a credit card is only when it is really necessary. Remember, your regular bills will always have to be paid. And buying on credit will cost you even more money in finance charges. So it is best to use it as little as possible.

Buying on credit is a good idea when:

1. you are buying something that you *really need*.

2. you can pay for what you've charged as soon as you get the bill.

3. you are taking advantage of a sale, but you don't have enough cash with you.

SHOULD I PAY CASH?

Some people should *not* buy on credit. These are people who don't keep careful track of their bills. They are surprised when their bills seem to suddenly add up and become unmanageable. These people are not responsible enough to use credit wisely. They often miss credit payments or fail to pay back their debts. All this information goes into their permanent credit file. In the future—even though they may have changed their ways—they will have trouble getting credit for anything.

Buying on credit is a bad idea when:

1. you make unnecessary purchases on impulse. (This means that you buy something just because you feel like it, with no thought for your budget.)

2. you already have to "juggle" all your credit payments. (This happens when you have charged too much in too many different places.)

3. you are unable to put any money into a savings account each month.

4. you often run out of money before payday arrives.

> **BEFORE USING A CREDIT CARD**
>
> ask yourself:
>
> - Can I easily do without this item?
>
> - Can I afford to pay for it?
>
> - Why not wait until I can pay cash?
>
> - When the bill comes, can I pay it off right away?

COMPREHENSION

Write **T** or **F** to show whether a statement is *true* or *false*. Write **NI** if there is *no information* in the reading to help you make a judgment.

1. _____ A credit card company charges no interest on bills paid within 30 days.

2. _____ Wise shoppers are surprised when their bills suddenly become unmanageable.

3. _____ A credit card company adds finance charges if you make only a partial payment.

4. _____ A bad credit record is erased once a teenager becomes an adult.

5. _____ If you don't keep careful track of your bills, you shouldn't use a credit card.

6. _____ Using as much credit as possible builds a good credit rating.

PUZZLER

Use the clues to help you solve the crossword puzzle.

ACROSS

1. intelligently; prudently

4. your plan for spending and saving

6. special time period when prices are reduced

7. describes expenses that must be paid every week or month

DOWN

2. a sudden, strong feeling that you want to do something

3. required; describes something you can't do without

5. to pay continual attention to what you're doing

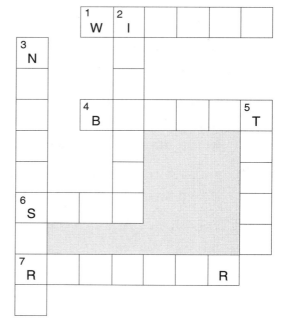

HOMOPHONES

Homophones are words that sound the same but have different meanings and spellings. First, underline the incorrect homophone in each phrase below. Then rewrite the phrase, using the correct homophone.

1. to by on credit _____

2. changed they're ways _____

3. bills have two be paid _____

4. pay four what you've charged _____

5. Can eye afford it? _____

6. people are knot responsible _____

7. charged to much _____

98

8. repay a lone _____

9. weight until later _____

10. with know thought for your budget _____

SYNONYMS

First, unscramble the words from the reading. Then write each word next to the phrase containing its *synonym* (word that means the same or almost the same).

PEPSHAN _____   SINGVAS _____

NITREETS _____   SACH _____

LILB _____   TUFRUE _____

1. your monthly **statement**

_____

2. in **years to come**

_____

3. **money put aside**

_____

4. **finance charges**

_____

5. **bills and coins**

_____

6. "juggling" **occurs** when

_____

WORD COMPLETION

Use vowels (*a, e, i, o, u*) to complete the words from the reading.

1. __ N M __ N __ G __ __ B L __

2. __ M P __ L S __

3. S __ V __ N G S __ C C __ __ N T

4. P __ Y D __ Y

5. __ F F __ R D

6. D __ S C __ P L __ N __

7. M __ T __ R __

8. B __ D G __ T

EXAMPLES

Circle a letter to show the correct answer to each question.

1. What kinds of items are people most likely to buy "on impulse"?

   a. fancy foods, expensive clothes
   b. bread, milk, paper towels
   c. pencils, binders, notebook paper

2. What is a sign of "financial discipline"?

   a. never going to malls or stores
   b. maintaining a regular system of saving
   c. eating just enough to stay alive

3. What could be a good way to control your use of credit?

   a. Count your money every night.
   b. Save all of your receipts.
   c. Leave your credit card at home.

PARTS OF SPEECH

A word's *part of speech* depends on how it is used in a sentence. Many words can be used as both nouns and verbs. Read the sentences below. Write **N** or **V** to show whether the **boldface** word is used as a *noun* or a *verb*. Then write a sentence of your own, using that word as the *other* part of speech. Remember that *nouns* name persons, places, or things. *Verbs* are words that show action or being.

1. I want to **cash** my paycheck at lunchtime. _____

   _____

2. How many **purchases** did you make today? _____

   _____

3. Don't **miss** any credit card payments. _____

   _____

4. **Can** you manage your money wisely? _____

_____

5. He got a good **buy** on his car. _____

_____

6. That interest **charge** is very high. _____

_____

SUFFIXES

First underline the word in each sentence that needs a *suffix* (word ending that changes its meaning). Then rewrite the word correctly on the line.

1. Can I easy do without this item?   _____

2. Keep track of your bills careful.   _____

3. Success money management takes discipline. _____

4. Don't miss any credit pay.   _____

ANTONYMS

Words from the reading are listed on the left. Draw a line to match each word with its *antonym* (word that means the opposite) on the right.

1. **necessary**   a. rarely

2. **suddenly**   b. gradually

3. **spend**   c. worst

4. **best**   d. save

5. **often**   e. optional

6. **arrive**   f. depart

BORROWING MONEY

Before reading . . .

It's always best to avoid borrowing money if you possibly can. But at some time you may have no choice. Perhaps you have a big, unexpected hospital bill to pay. Or you may need to buy a new car or a house. In these situations, most people must take out a loan.

Always shop around before you take out a loan. Try to get the lowest rates possible. Banks often offer loans at fairly high rates. A savings and loan association may offer slightly lower rates. And the rates of credit unions may be even lower.

You can apply for a loan directly at a bank or a savings and loan. Or you may be able to join a credit union through your place of business, your labor union, or your church. Then, as a member, you can apply for a loan. But make sure you only join an *insured* credit union. You will want to be sure that your money is protected.

Only borrow money from a lender you know something about. If you're in doubt, ask the Better Business Bureau. Most credit unions are well run, but others are not. The Better Business Bureau maintains records of consumers' complaints.

Try to avoid private finance companies. These firms lend money, but they charge very high rates. They also charge very stiff penalties for late payments. Some private finance companies have very bad reputations.

Before you take out a loan, ask an expert for advice. You might also read books about borrowing money. If you must take out a loan, you should be prepared and well-informed before doing so.

Loans are complicated. If your loan application is approved, you must sign a contract. This is a legal document. Your signature means that you have agreed to all its terms.

You should always read any loan contract closely. It will state all the terms of the loan. These terms will include the following:

1. the amount of the loan

2. the length of time you have to pay back the loan

3. the yearly percentage rate (the interest charged each year)

4. the total cost of the loan (the amount of the loan plus the total interest charged)

5. the payment rate (how much you have to pay when each payment is due)

The contract will also state penalties. Penalties are charged if you are late making your payments. Read the terms of the contract carefully. You may find it is better *not* to take out the loan.

Never sign a contract until you have read it completely—including the fine print. What are *all* the terms of the agreement? Get expert advice if you don't understand the terms.

The cost of a loan will vary. It will depend on three things: first, the amount of the loan; second, the rate of interest charged by the lender; and third, the length of time you have to pay back the loan. Look at the chart below. It shows what a $1,000 loan could cost at different interest rates over different time periods. Notice how big the differences can really be.

ANNUAL PERCENTAGE RATE	LENGTH OF LOAN (IN MONTHS)	MONTHLY PAYMENTS	FINANCE CHARGE	TOTAL COST
9.25%	6	$182.08	$ 92.50	$1092.50
	12	98.75	185.00	1,185.00
	24	49.38	277.50	1,277.50
	36	38.05	370.00	1,370.00
12%	6	186.67	120.00	1,120.00
	12	93.34	240.00	1,240.00
	24	61.67	480.00	1,480.00
	36	47.78	720.00	1,720.00
15%	6	191.67	150.00	1,150.00
	12	95.84	300.00	1,300.00
	24	66.67	600.00	1,600.00
	36	52.78	900.00	1,900.00
18%	6	196.67	180.00	1,180.00
	12	98.34	360.00	1,360.00
	24	64.17	540.00	1,540.00
	36	52.78	900.00	1,900.00

COMPREHENSION

Write **T** or **F** to show whether a statement is *true* or *false*. Write **NI** if there is *no information* in the reading to help you make a judgment.

1. _____ The Better Business Bureau keeps records of complaints made by banks and credit unions.

2. _____ Private finance companies usually charge very high rates.

3. _____ Do not sign a loan application unless you agree with its terms.

4. _____ All businesses establish credit unions for their employees.

5. _____ Savings and loan associations charge fewer penalties than banks do.

6. _____ The larger your monthly payments, the quicker your loan will be repaid.

SYLLABLES

Break the following words into syllables (separate sounds).

1. annual

_____/_____/_____

2. borrowing

_____/_____/_____

3. financial

_____/_____/_____

4. possibly

_____/_____/_____

5. consumers

_____/_____/_____

6. complicated

_____/_____/_____/_____

7. unexpected

_____/_____/_____/_____

8. preparation

_____/_____/_____/_____

9. reputation

_____/_____/_____/_____

10. situations

_____/_____/_____/_____

PUZZLER

Use the clues to help you solve the crossword puzzle.

ACROSS

1. a person who buys a product or service

4. approximately every four weeks; 12 times a year

6. the conditions of a contract or agreement

DOWN

1. written agreement that one can be held to by law

2. group of people joined together for a common purpose

3. certain sum of money

5. name for the type of union formed among fellow workers with the same trade or employer

VOCABULARY

Study the **boldface** words from the reading. Then draw a line to match each word with its *antonym* (word with the opposite meaning).

1. **legal**

2. **prepared**

3. **approved**

4. **lend**

a. borrow

b. rejected

c. unready

d. unlawful

PLURALS

Study the words from the reading. Write each word in its *plural* (names more than one) form.

1. reputation _____

2. penalty _____

3. charge _____

4. contract _____

5. company _____

6. church _____

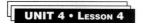

FORMS OF A WORD

Notice that the **boldface** word in each sentence is in the wrong *form*.
Rewrite each sentence on the line, using the correct form.

1. You must fill out an **apply** before you will be considered for a loan.

   _____

2. The Better Business Bureau **maintenance** records of consumers' complaints.

   _____

3. Make sure you join an **insuring** credit union.

   _____

4. A savings and loan association may offer **slight** lower rates.

   _____

5. The rates charged by credit unions may be the **lower** of all.

   _____

6. You may be **ability** to join a credit union through your church.

   _____

7. Read the terms of the contract **careful**

   _____

8. What is the **lengthy** of time you have to repay the loan?

   _____

9. You should never sign a contract until you have read it **complete**.

   _____

10. The cost of a loan will **dependently** on several things.

   _____

SYNONYMS

Choose a *synonym* (word with the same or almost the same meaning) from the box for the **boldface** word or words in each sentence. Write the synonyms on the lines. Hint: You will *not* use all the words in the box.

unsure of	yearly	annual	monthly	moderate
certain of	differ	high	opinion	thoroughly

1. Never sign a contract until you have read it **completely**. _____

2. If you're **doubtful about** a lender, check it out with the Better Business Bureau. _____

3. Look for the lowest **annual** percentage rate being offered. _____

4. Before you take out a loan, get the **advice** of an expert. _____

5. Private finance companies charge very **stiff** penalties. _____

6. The cost of a loan will **vary** for three reasons. _____

7. You must be **sure of** your ability to meet the terms of a loan agreement. _____

READING A CHART

Use information from the chart to complete the sentences.

1. The lowest total cost of a $1,000 loan is _____ if the loan is repaid in _____ months.

2. The highest total cost of a $1,000 loan is _____ if the loan is repaid in _____ months.

VOCABULARY

Unscramble the words to complete the sentences.

1. If your income and outgo are the same, your budget is

   CLEANDAB _____.

2. It takes **CLIPSIDINE** _____ to use a credit card

   responsibly.

3. You must list all your sources of **NOMICE** _____

   on your credit application.

4. Signing a loan **TONCCRAT** _____ means that

   you agree with all of its terms.

MULTIPLE CHOICE

Circle a letter to show how each sentence should be completed.

1. The main thing a creditor wants to know is

   a. how well you can
      manage money.

   b. how long you have
      lived in your house.

   c. whether you are single,
      married, or divorced.

   d. whether or not you've
      ever been arrested.

2. You can avoid paying finance charges if you

   a. pay for your purchases
      with cash.

   b. make the minimum
      monthly payments.

   c. pay the entire balance
      every month.

   d. both a and c

3. The total cost of a loan includes

   a. yearly percentage and
      payment rate.

   b. amount of the loan plus
      total interest charged.

   c. length of the loan
      and percentage rate.

   d. the application and
      the contract.

GLOSSARY OF READING TERMS

adapted rewritten to be made shorter or easier to read

alliteration repetition of the initial sound in two or more words; a poetic device

analyze to identify and examine the separate parts of a whole

author's purpose the writer's specific goal or reason for writing a particular book, article, etc.

categorize to divide into main subjects or groups

cause a happening or situation that makes something else happen as a result

classify to organize according to some similarity

compare to make note of how two or more things are alike

compound word a word made by combining two or more words

conclusion the end or last part of a novel, article, etc.

context clues the words in a sentence just before and after an unfamiliar word or phrase. Context clues help to make clear what the unfamiliar word means.

contrast to make note of how two or more things are different from one another

describe to tell or write about something or someone in detail in order to help the reader or listener create a mental image

details bits of information or description that support the main idea and make it clearer

dialogue lines spoken by characters in a story or play

discuss to talk or write about a topic, giving various opinions and ideas

effect the reaction or impact that occurs as a result of a cause

elements the essential parts or components of a whole

excerpt section quoted from a book, article, etc.

fact something that actually happened or is really true

fiction literary work in which the plot and characters are imagined by the author

figurative language colorful, nonliteral use of words and phrases to achieve a dramatic effect

generalize to form a general rule or idea after considering particular facts

graphs charts or diagrams that visually present changes in something or the relationship between two or more changing things

homonyms words pronounced alike but having different meanings and usually different spellings

identify to name or point out; to distinguish someone or something from others

image idea, impression; a picture in the mind

inference conclusion arrived at by careful reasoning

interpret to explain the meaning of; to figure out in one's own way

judgment a decision made after weighing various facts

literature the entire body of written work including fiction, nonfiction, drama, poetry, etc.

locate find; tell where something is

main idea the point or central thought in a written work or part of a work

multiple-meaning words lookalike words that have different meanings in different contexts

nonfiction writing about the real world, real people, actual events, etc.

objective reflecting what is actual or real; expressed without bias or opinion

order items arranged or sequenced in a certain way, such as alphabetical order or order of importance

organize to put in place according to a system

outcome the result; the way that something turns out

parts of speech grammatical classifications of eight word types: adjective, adverb, conjunction, interjection, noun, preposition, pronoun, or verb

passage section of a written work

plot the chain of events in a story that leads to the story's outcome

plural word form showing more than one person, place, or thing

point of view the position from which something is observed or told; when a character tells the story, *first person* point of view is used; an author who tells the story in his own voice is using *third person* point of view.

predict to foretell what you think will happen in the future

prefix group of letters added at the beginning of a word to change the word's meaning or function

recall to remember or bring back to mind

refer to speak of something or call attention to it

relationship a connection of some kind between two or more persons, things, events, etc.

scan to glance at something or look over it quickly

sequence items in order; succession; one thing following another

singular word form naming just one person, place, or thing

subjective reflecting personal ideas, opinions, or experiences

suffix group of letters added at the end of a word that changes the word's meaning or function

symbol a concrete object used to represent an abstract idea

table an orderly, graphic arrangement of facts, figures, etc.

tense verb form that shows the time of the action, such as past, present, or future

term word or phrase with a special meaning in a certain field of study such as art, history, etc.

tone the feeling given by the author's choice of language

vocabulary all the words of a language